# BLACK MARKET OPERATIONS

*MARKETING THEORY*
*AND THE FENCING OF STOLEN GOODS*

A Report By

Ted Roselius, Associate Professor
Douglas Benton, Associate Professor

COLLEGE OF BUSINESS
COLORADO STATE UNIVERSITY
FORT COLLINS, COLORADO

LOOMPANICS UNLIMITED

Much of the information in **BLACK MARKET OPERATIONS** is extracted from LEAA report No. NI 70-065-PG-10, "Marketing Theory and the Fencing of Stolen Goods," produced by Professors Ted Roselius and Doug Benton of the College of Business, Colorado State University, under a grant from the Law Enforcement Assistance Administration. For this new edition, we have edited the text, retypeset, and added new material.



**LOOMPANICS UNLIMITED**
**PO BOX 1197**
**PORT TOWNSEND, WA 98368**


**ISBN: 1-55950-017-4**
**Library of Congress**
**Card Catalog Number 89-045800**

# PREFACE TO THE LOOMPANICS EDITION

*"Black Market: a place or system for selling goods illegally".*
*-WEBSTER'S NEW WORLD DICTIONARY*

Governments have always interfered with free trade among their citizens. That's what a government is -- an agency which uses force to snoop into other people's business.

They always give noble motives for doing so. You seldom hear a politician or bureaucrat *say* he wants to restrict trade so he can preserve a monopoly for a special interest who has contributed to his campaign. Nor do you often hear one say that he wants absolute control over every exchange you make so he can make you pay taxes on everything you do. No, they always *say* it is "necessary" to restrict *your* freedom of choice in order to "protect the national interest". or some other nebulous concept.

It's all crap, of course. Many libertarian authors, most notably Murray Rothbard in his *POWER AND MARKET*, have refuted *all* government rationalizations for snooping into your business.

While much has been written about free market economics on the theoretical level, little has been written on the *practice* of free trade in an unfree (i.e., government regulated) economy. People who engage in illegal transactions usually keep their mouths shut about it, with the result that anyone interested in *practicing* free trade (and not just talking about it) has little material available for study.

As part of our effort to disseminate information on how black markets actually operate, we are proud to present this study by Professors Roselius and Benton. This book focuses on one particular illegal market -- the traffic in stolen goods.

We do not mean to encourage traffic in stolen property. Rather, we wish to encourage *honest* trade among free men. The traffic in stolen goods does, however, present an actual black market which has operated since time immemorial in spite of all government efforts to stop it. One does not have to be a thief or fence to benefit from this study. The general principles set forth can be adapted to any other illegal or "black" market -- drugs, gasoline ration coupons, or any other restricted commodity or service. The reader should emphasize *principles* rather than *particulars* in his study of this material.

The authors do not engage in moral denunciations. Instead, they take an *economic* approach in dealing with the problems of pricing, marketing, distribution, storage, and other business aspects of dealing in illegal commodities.

Free men have always found ways of dealing with each other to their mutual satisfaction, and it is hoped that the principles of black market operations revealed in this book will serve that end. When governments develop the maturity to allow freedom of economic acts between consenting adults, then a knowledge of black market operations will be of academic interest only. Until then, freedom of choice exists only for those who seek it.

-Michael Hoy, Publisher

TABLE OF CONTENTS

# PREFACE

The research reported here was supported by the National Institute of Law Enforcement and Criminal Justice, Law Enforcement Assistance Administration, U.S. Department of Justice, and the College of Business, Colorado State University. The research was conducted as part of the Pilot Grant Program under Institute Grant Number NI-70-065-PG-10 from June 1970 to August 1971.

The purpose of this research is to explore the feasibility of using conventional marketing theory as a basis for understanding the behavior of thieves and fences as they conduct traffic in stolen property. A discussion of sources and specific recommendations are included. The study also serves as the foundation for design of specific methods for reducing the traffic in stolen goods. This pilot study provides basic information necessary to begin a scientific analysis of the distribution of stolen goods.

The research team gratefully acknowledges the assistance provided by numerous law enforcement officials, convicts and exconvicts, businessmen and others whose willingness to tell us about various elements of fencing was so necessary to the completion of the study. Additional acknowledgement is given to the National Institute for their guidance and to the administration and faculty of the College of Business for their moral support.

# SUMMARY

*Marketing theory offers a framework for visualizing the traffic in stolen property. Many concepts from marketing theory can be utilized for blocking and investigating stolen goods traffic and can provide substantial enrichment to other investigative approaches.*

Current knowledge of the traffic in stolen goods is composed of unconnected observations about widely scattered events. There is no operational scheme for visualizing diverse activities or for relating observations to each other. Perhaps in no other area are observations as seemingly random and meaningless as are the various observations about thieves and fences. In no other area are investigators so hampered by the lack of a theoretical framework that would add perspective to their investigations as are those who investigate traffic in stolen property. Marketing theory can provide the needed perspective.

The purpose of a theory is to polarize the scatter of events and to crystallize individual observations into a complete description of the whole. A theory on the traffic in stolen goods would allow an investigator to understand and to predict the behavior of thieves and fences.

This project is an exploratory study to determine the feasibility of using conventional marketing theory as an operational scheme for visualizing the traffic in stolen goods. It concludes that legitimate marketing theory can serve as the foundation for building a "theory of distribution for stolen property". Such a theory is necessary if law enforcement officials are to make substantial advances in blocking and investigating the traffic in stolen goods.

Thieves and fences make significant marketing oriented decisions as they conduct the distribution of stolen goods. They face many of the same problems a legitimate businessman faces as he matches supply and demand. They can be expected to use many of the same strategies and procedures in solving those problems.

Marketing theory is a collection of thoughts which describes the operation and institutions used to execute a marketing program. This theory has been used to explain and understand distribution activities in widely varied and complex settings.

The amount of disequilibrium between the demand for and the supply of particular kinds of stolen goods in a market area will have an impact on the behavior of thieves and fences. Monitoring of this equilibrium by law enforcement officials will provide enough information to allow law enforcement agencies to predict actions taken by fences, thus permitting substantial progress in deterring and investigating the traffic.

As thieves and fences attempt to match the demand and supply of stolen property, they must give careful consideration to the buying motives and buying habits of the consumers they serve. To the extent that law enforcement officials can learn the socioeconomic descriptions of the customers of thieves or fences, they can gain valuable insights about the operations of thieves and fences.

The process of serving as a middleman in the distribution of stolen goods is a very complex one requiring rational decision making by thieves and fences. Each function -- buying, selling, transporting, storing, financing, risk taking, information gathering, and standardization -- is subject to study by law enforcement agencies. Further study would isolate those functions which are vulnerable to deterrence and investigation.

A rational distribution of stolen merchandise requires a complete and integrated marketing management program. This program is composed of a mix of decisions in the areas of channel of distribution, price, promotion, and product design which must fit the unique buying motives and habits of the fences's market segment. When thieves or fences sell to unaware buyers of stolen property they must undertake some effort to legitimize the transaction. If a fence is distributing to heavy users of stolen goods, his price, promotion, and channel of distribution will reflect the fact.

This initial and exploratory investigation of the feasibility of applying marketing theory to understand traffic in stolen property suggests several policies and strategies useful in blocking that flow. The traffic in stolen goods is deterred to the extent that the channel of distribution can be lengthened. The ability to block the traffic in stolen goods increases as the supply of stolen goods becomes greater than demand. Any action that increases the price of stolen goods provides a substantial barrier to the flow. Many additional strategies and procedures are detailed in the text of the report.

The study also indicates that investigatory models can be designed to provide substantial assistance to investigators. A continuous monitoring of the state of disequilibrium between demand and supply will make isolated case facts much more meaningful. Improved incident reporting, statistical analyses of those reports, and communication of data between jurisdictions are absolute necessities and will provide, among other things, significant increases in understanding the traffic in stolen goods. Additional investigatory models are explained in the text.

Additional research is required in order to make an operational adaptation of conventional marketing theory to the unique situations found in the distribution of stolen goods. Further study outlined in the text will isolate additional strategies and procedures that would be effective in blocking and investigating the flow of stolen goods.

Efforts of law enforcement agencies are most effective when they are tailored to fit the differences in the marketing programs of the thieves and fences. Thus, law enforcement officials would benefit from a consideration of conventional marketing theory and from training investigators in marketing concepts.

# CHAPTER 1

## INTRODUCTION

*"Professional crime would not exist except for two essential relationships with legitimate society: the 'fence' and the 'fix'."*

*-President's Commission on Law Enforcement and Administration of Justice, THE CHALLENGE OF CRIME IN A FREE SOCIETY.*

For some time, psychologists have studied the criminal as an individual. Thus, we have studies on the motivation, attitudes, personality and other aspects of the criminal mind. These studies have led to advances in the areas of rehabilitation, deterrence, and occasionally in investigation.

Also, sociologists have treated crime as an anomaly of the social structure of society, and have studied the social organization of gangs, the impact of crime on social values, the social factors leading to a criminal career, and other important questions.

In contrast, the approach of the present study is to visualize the distribution of stolen goods as a legitimate business and marketing problem. An underlying concept of this study is that professional crime is organized on an economic basis rather than entirely on a sociological or psychological base. The approach is that of assuming that much of the crime dealing with property is organized and operated on the same basis as a legitimate business, with about the same objectives (profit) and many of the same problems in reaching that objective. If the assumption is feasible, we could reasonably expect the fence and the thief to use many of the same marketing techniques to solve the problems he faces in distributing stolen property.

There is a body of knowledge available for describing and predicting the behavior of persons involved in the legitimate distribution of goods. If there is any commonality of behavior, between legitimate and criminal marketing, this knowledge may be usable for predicting the behavior of thieves and fences.

It should be clear that this line of investigation is a supplement to other approaches, and certainly is not a substitute for them. In fact, we found many decisions being made on psychological bases as well as economic ones. For instance, one interviewee simply could not stand the face-to-face contact required for some forms of theivery (checks, stick up) and stayed strictly with burglary and larceny for personality reasons, not economic reasons. However, we did also find many decisions being made on the basis of economic criteria. For example, several interviewees preferred jewelry and fur thefts over larger chattels because of the lower risks in theft and the ease of storage, high rates of turnover, and high markup, which are marketing reasons, not psychological nor sociological reasons.

To visualize the professional, organized distribution of stolen property as if it were a business-like operation, we see a major division of the problem into two areas: (1) the *production* of stolen property, accomplished by the theft activity, and (2) the *marketing or distribution* of stolen property as accomplished by fences and other middlemen. Any business faces the same two broad categories of problems.

The "production" side has been studied extensively, resulting in new kinds of alarms, locks, secuirty devices and theft-detection systems. The "distribution" side is relatively untouched by formal research. To study the marketing side of the problem we make the assumption that the distribution of stolen property is rather business-like, perhaps more so than the production side, and assume that many patterns of behavior in distribution are *economically* motivated.

The "fence" is defined as any individual who knowingly buys stolen property and thereby is subject to prosecution as a receiver of stolen goods. "Fencing" is the process of buying, receiving or otherwise trafficking in stolen goods for any purpose.

*What Is Marketing?*

In the conventional view, marketing is defined as "the performance of business activities that direct the flow of goods and services from producer to consumer or user."(1) This definition gives some justification for viewing the theft of goods as "production" and the fencing of goods as "marketing". However, a broader definition is often used to give more specific direction to the persons charged with performing the marketing functions. Thus, "Marketing is a total system of interacting business activities designed to plan, price, promote, and distribute want-satisfying products and services to present and potential users."(2) This definition allows one to assume that much of the behavior found in the distribution of stolen goods consists of rational, economically guided decisions. It also indicates that the distribution requires conscious effort and decision making by the thief and fence -- it does not "just happen automatically." Still another source defines marketing as "all activities intended to stimulate or serve demand,"(3) to more clearly distinguish marketing from production.

In the present context then, marketing refers to all the activities performed and the treatment given to stolen property between the time it is stolen and the time it is eventually consumed. Thus, a study of the marketing of stolen goods would include transactions between thief and fence, the amount and kind of demand for stolen property, prices received for stolen property, promotion technique, behavior of middlemen, buying motives and habits of the consumer of stolen goods, and many other related topics.

Historically, there have been many approaches to the study of marketing.[4] The "commodity approach" takes one commodity, apples for instance, and studies each of the elements involved in distribution of that commodity. The "management approach" studies each of the managerial decisions that must be made by persons involved in various marketing activities. The "comparative approach" simply compares marketing practices in various settings, usually different countries.[5] Clearly, the approach used in this project is a combination of the commodity, comparative, and managerial approaches. We work with one commodity (stolen goods), and study the economic and managerial behavior of thieves and fences by comparing them with what a legitimate businessman would do in the same situation.

"Marketing theory" is the collection of principles and models which have been reported to be useful in studying the practices of persons involved in the distribution of goods, in studying the structure of organizations and institutions involved in the distribution, and in studying the patterns for flow of goods. Since the literature on marketing is voluminous, we have abstracted some of the more basic, general, and communicable concepts from this literature.

It is reasonable to expect that portions of the legitimate theory would change when certain constraints are lifted. The most significant constraint removed by using marketing theory in the present context is that here there is not a definite relationship between the cost of an item and the price asked for it. The two major costs not fully incurred by our subjects are cost of goods sold and taxes. Other constraints which face legitimate marketers but not thieves and fences are laws covering restraint of trade, trade practices, weights and measures, honor of warranty, labeling, packaging, zoning, and so on. Where these points are relevant they will be mentioned.

Certainly, all of the following concepts taken together do not constitute a complete marketing theory. Further, some of the concepts are borrowed freely from the related disciplines of economics, psychology, management, and sociology, as is the common practice in marketing literature. They do illustrate major elements of a unique set of behavior that is worthy of further study.

*The Research Question*

The objective of this research project is to answer the following questions:

(1) Are professional thieves and fences in any way similar in their marketing behavior to legimate businessmen?
(2) Can legitimate marketing theory serve as a vehicle for describing the behavior of thieves and fences in their distribution of stolen property?
(3) Can conventional marketing theory provide a significant assist in investigating and deterring the traffic in stolen property?

*Value Of This Approach*

Positive answers to these questions would yield substantial and direct benefit in at least two areas:

(1) *Creation of blocking strategies* -- steps taken by law enforcement departments to make the distribution of stolen goods so expensive, time consuming, or risky that there would be a significant lessening of the incentive to deal with stolen goods.

(2) Design of *investigatory stragegies* -- systematic ways of visualizing the activities related to the traffic in stolen goods. Not only would such a framework make case evidence more meaningful to the investigator, it would allow him to predict the existence of activities and instutions before actual facts are available. This would allow an investigator to short-cut the tortuous chain of obscure clues by predicting activities most likely to be occurring.

*Research Approach and Methodology*

The underlying thought in designing a research approach was that this was to be an exploratory project, investigating only the *feasibility* of applying marketing theory to a new problem area. It was necessary for researchers knowledgeable in marketing to become familiar with some of the practices of thieves and fences as well as with some of the problems and practices of law enforcement.

Thus, the general research approach was as follows:

(1) Interview a sampling of thieves and fences to become workably familiar with the distribution of stolen goods.

(2) Select illustrative marketing theories seemingly most descriptive of the behavior, and adapt them to fit instances uncovered during the interviews.

(3) Interview a sampling of law enforcement personnel to determine the problems

they face and whether new ways of thinking would add to their investigative or deterring power.

*Limitations and Scope*

There are four major limitations on the scope of this study:

(1) The scope of this study is primarily limited to what happens to goods *after* the thievery, rather than with elements of the burglary or larceny itself.

(2) We are concerned primarily with the instances where goods are stolen for resale or exchange, and not with cases where goods are taken for use by the thief, or thefts occuring during vandalism, petty shoplifting, and the like. This limitation results from our definition of a "professional thief" as one who steals for the sole purpose of converting the goods into cash. The professional may be a "loner" working independently of others, or he may be a member of any one of several kinds of criminal organizations.

(3) We are concerned only with the case where there is some *regularity* of the thieving and fencing activity. This is due to our definition of "organized" crime as being a systematic operation providing a relatively continuous flow of stolen goods.

(4) The conclusions we draw are based on *sample information* rather than on a complete enumeration of all situations. Since this is an exploratory project, we could not afford the luxury of using sophisticated methods of collecting a scientifically random sample of information. For the purposes here, we believe it is entirely appropriate to use illustrative cases whose authenticity may not be of courtroom

trial quality. For instance, some of the sample of information we use would be regarded as heresay, second hand reports. However, we feel this is not a severe restriction on drawing conclusions.

*Importance of Limitation Number Four* -- Because this is an exploratory research project, limitation number four has special significance.

The general hypothesis of the project is that conventional marketing theory is a feasible method of study to provide an understanding of the traffic in stolen property. As stated above, the test of this hypothesis is made with a sample of information. Because the test is based on sample information, the test could result in any one of the following conclusions:

(1) The correct conclusion could be made. The correct decision may be either to accept the hypothesis *if* the marketing theory approach is valid, or to reject the hypothesis *if* the approach is not valid.

(2) A Type I error could be made. This would occur if one rejected the hypothesis (concluded that marketing theory is not effective), when in reality it is true (the approach would have been effective). If this kind of error was made, an opportunity would be missed to use a viable method of studying the problem.

(3) A Type II error could be made. This would occur if one accepted the hypothesis (concluded that marketing theory is an effective vehicle) when in reality it is not true (the approach proves ineffective). If this error was made, the approach would be tried later and proved to be ineffective.

A jury faces much the same problem. On the

basis of a sample of evidence they must decide the guilt or innocence of a person. Their hypotheses is that the man is innocent. A correct decision would be either to hang the man if he is guilty, or to free him if he is innocent. A Type I error would be to hang an innocent man. A Type II error would be to free a guilty man.

As is detailed elsewhere in this report, it is our decision to accept the hypothesis of the legitimacy of marketing theory as an instrument of law enforcement on the basis of sample information. We believe legitimate marketing theory is a viable structure for studying some important aspects of certain kinds of distribution of stolen property.

Therefore, since we accept the hypothesis we have either made the correct decision, or else a Type II error. Unfortunately, in this case and in every other case where a decision is made on the basis of sample information, we will not know whether the correct decision or an error has been made until it is "too late" in light of future events. While we are subjectively confident of having made the correct decision, there is no way to assess the probabilities of having made the correct decision, since the sample information is not quantifiable.

*Organization Of This Report*

The report is written for an audience assumed to be very familiar with practices of law enforcement and whose knowledge of marketing concepts are no more than the casual observations of a layman. Chapter II provides basic marketing concepts and illustrates how they might be applied to the study of Traffic in Stolen Goods. Chapter III includes summaries of information from sources studied for this project. Finally, Chapter IV presents conclusions and recommendations in the form of blocking strategies, investigatory models and suggestions for additional research.

# CHAPTER II

## MARKETING OF STOLEN PROPERTY

The present chapter is divided into major sections on demand and supply, marketing processes, functions of middlemen and marketing management, and accompanying analyses for traffic in stolen goods.

### DEMAND AND SUPPLY

This section, like subsequent major divisions, follows a pattern of discussing the general concept first, and then providing applications of the concept for stolen property.

*Theory of Demand and Supply*

The quantity demanded of an item is a function of its price, the seller's promotion efforts, and the buyer's ability to buy as limited by his income. For instance, practically all products have a relationship between price and the quantity sold, as shown by line D in the following graph. The law of downward sloping demand states that as the price of an item is decreased, more of it will be demanded and sold.

Price elasticity of demand is an indicator of the degree to which quantity sold responds to a change in price. The elasticity coefficient has a range from zero to infinity. A coefficient less than 1 indicates that a decrease in price will not be compensated for by the resulting increase in quantity sold;

thus, in this case of *inelastic* demand, total revenue decreases with a price decrease. A coefficient greater than 1 indicates that a decrease in price will be more than offset by an increase in quantity sold; in this case of *elastic* demand, total revenue increases with a drop in price.

Three of the most common types of elasticity are: (1) price elasticity, showing the responsiveness of quantity sold to changes in price; (2) promotional elasticity, showing the responsiveness to changes in the amount of promotion; and (3) income elasticity, showing the responsiveness in quantity sold to changes in the level of income of the potential buyers.

Demand is also considered to be either "primary" (desire for coffee) or "selective" (desire to buy a specific brand of coffee). Both types of demand must be present before a sale can be made. Thus, a fence selling stolen goods to a person hesitant to buy stolen goods knowingly, must first overcome the hesitancy to buy *any* stolen goods (create primary demand) and then convince him to buy the specific items offered for sale.

The aggregate supply of an item offered for sale is a function of all costs involved in producing that item and the price for which it can be sold. The price relationship can be shown as a line, S, on the following graph.

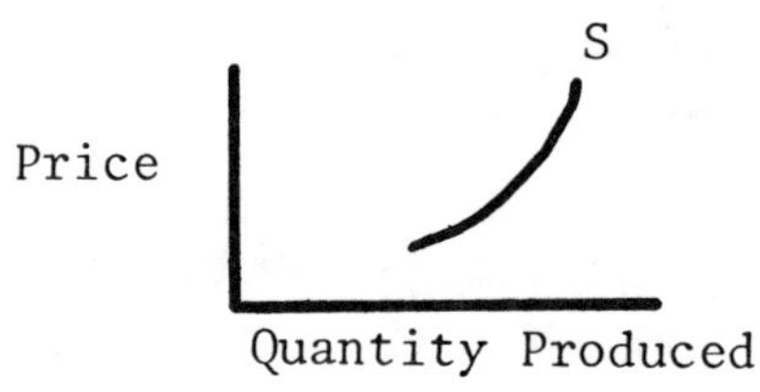


As the price of an item drops, the aggregate quantity supplied will drop accordingly, assuming costs of production are constant.

Equilibrium between quantity sold and quantity demanded is achieved when the buyers and sellers agree on a market price. The market price results in equilibrium between supply and demand, and determines the volume of goods traded, as shown by P (market price) and Q (volume traded) in the following graph.

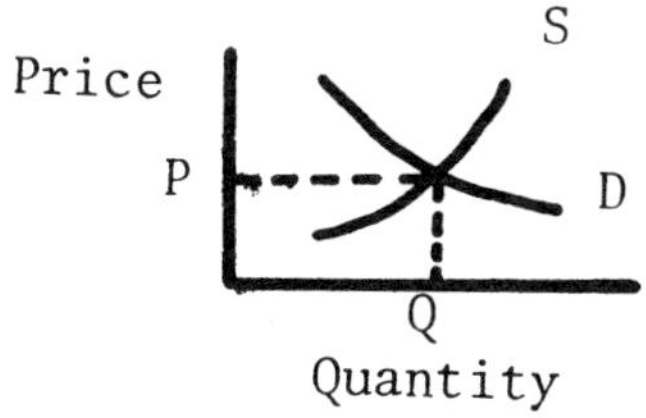


The conventional wisdom of economics indicates an "automatic" movement toward equilibrium brought about by competition, free movement of prices, and entry and exit of firms from the market. However, a formalized marketing system is required to equalize local differences between demand and supply.

We can distinguish between three special kinds of market economies: (1) a "black market" operating in an economy of scarcity; (2) a "market for stolen goods" operating in an economy of abundance; and (3) a market for illegal items operating in an open economy. In an economy of scarcity a rationing system and price controls are used to provide some semblance of equilibrium.(1) The fact that demand is greater than the supply of goods will drive the price of goods to an "artificially" high level (above equilibrium), creating a "black market" in which goods move illegally at prices above the official price and in quantities not authorized by the rationing system. In an economy of abundance, there is a market comparable to the black market. In this report, we refer to this market as the "market for stolen goods", consisting of stolen items moving through illegal channels. A major distinction between the black market and the market for stolen goods is that prices are higher than the official market price in the former, and lower than the regular price in the latter. Finally, there may be an economy with a market for illegal items, such as narcotics, moonshine liquor, or prostitutes, for which there is not a normal, open market, and in which illegal items move at a market price which equates supply and demand.

The general level of disequilibrium between supply and demand determines whether there is a "seller's market" in which supply is less than demand, where the supplier need not stimulate demand because he has the balance of negotiating power, the supplier has few problems of selling, and is able to name the price; or whether there is a "buyer's market" in which demand is less than supply and the sellers must compete with each other in persuading the potential buyers by elaborate systems of marketing (including the creation of selective demand through advertising, product differentiation and other marketing activities).

*Demand and Supply of Stolen Property*

One could assume the demand curve for stolen goods to be price inelastic, even though most of the demand is created because the seller is able to ask a substantially lower price. However, the risk and inconvenience of buying stolen goods is so great that a substantial price drop is probably required to generate more sales. Thus, the demand curve for stolen goods is to the left of and below the regular demand as shown in the following graph.

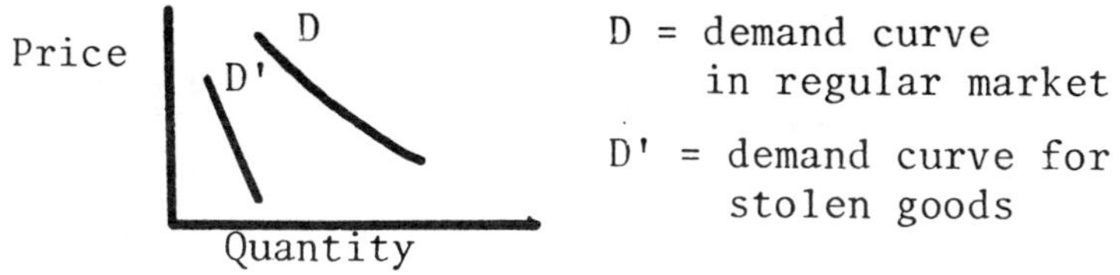


Since the product has such a strong price appeal, one would also expect the products to be highly elastic relative to the income level of the consumer. As a person's income level becomes lower, the price appeal becomes even more substantial because the price savings are more important. We would also expect the demand to be very promotion elastic, since very little promotion is done because of the difficulty of promotion. Thus, a little bit of promotion by the thief would probably reach new potential markets of substantial size.

However, the general demand characteristics for stolen goods probably varies with both the market segment and with the type of goods. If items are extremely hot, for instance very traceable artwork, the buyer takes on substantial risk and the seller is giving up substantial risk. This would give the buyer a negotiating advantage associated with a buyer's market, and yield a low price. If the items are more widely marketable, due to a larger or more diverse potential market, demand is increased and the seller gains negotiating strength, yielding a higher price.

Primary demand for stolen goods is probably relatively low in the public at large, but may be very high within certain low-income sectors of the population. However, one could assume that the primary demand for stolen goods would increase with an overall increase in theft rate, with a decline in the social taboos of associating with shady characters, and with increased social mobility, even though an increase in average income would make stolen goods less desirable. Thus, the stolen goods marketer is not faced with a severe problem of having to stimulate primary demand. However, as the volume of stolen goods increases, one would expect increased efforts to promote selective demand as thieves begin to compete with each other and with legitimate dealers for the market. In short, theives and fences are under increasing pressure to become marketing oriented.

The supply of stolen goods is probably price inelastic. In the short run the thief probably determines his quantity stolen more by opportunity factors than by the current market price of the item compared to what the price has been and because he does not have to be concerned about production costs. Also, the aggregate supply curve is considerably lower than the supply curve for the item in the legitimate market due to the smaller number of producers, as shown in the following graph.

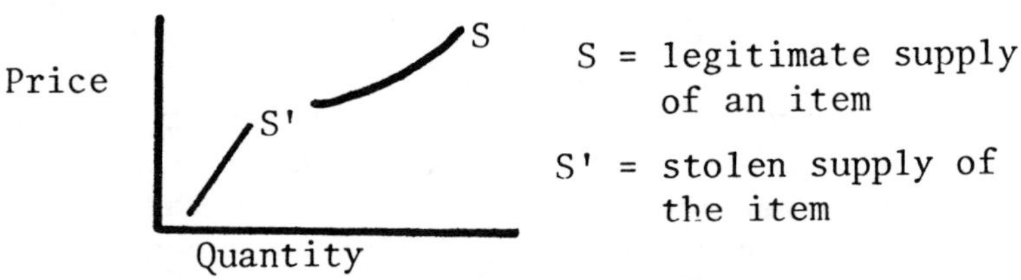


Over a short period of time (perhaps a year), one would expect the demand for stolen goods to be reasonably stable in a market area, although a prolonged strike or massive layoff would create a temporary increase in demand. However, the supply of stolen goods is probably a very volatile thing, being upset by either a large theft of an item or a large recovery by the police. A large theft would shift the supply curve to the right.

One would expect that at any one point in time there would be somewhat of an equilibrium between the supply of and the demand for a given type of stolen good in a geographical market area. However, one or two large burglaries or hijackings in a city may provide an unmanageable surplus of the item in that market. Since both supply and demand are fairly inelastic, a small shift in the supply curve has a profound impact on the equilibrium price, as shown on the following graph.

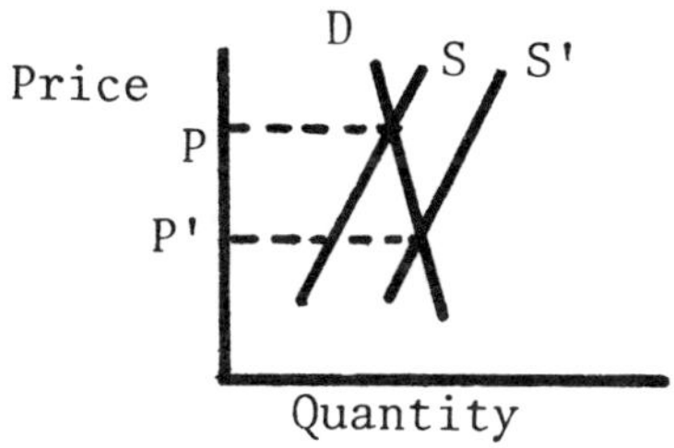


A cargo theft of the item shifts supply curve to S', and equilibrium price drops to P'. In this case, either one of three things would occur. An equilibrium between supply and demand could be re-established simply by a decrease in the price asked by the seller. Or equilibrium could be re-established by transporting the surplus items to another market region. Finally, it could be re-established by tapping into a new market segment such as selling to the next most risky market which may be the legitimate channels.

Analysis of the state of equilibrium between supply and demand in a local market provides opportunities to law enforcement agencies. A continuous interdepartmental monitoring of supply and demand would provide operational information about the flow of goods. For instance, sales of stolen goods to a higher income group would indicate price of the item is higher and reflects a lower supply of that item in the one geographical area. One could expect an entrepreneur to either import more of the goods or to have more of them stolen.

## THE MARKETING PROCESS

### *Assortments of Goods: Matching Supply With Demand*

Never will a producer of goods produce in exactly the quantities or assortments needed by potential customers. Nor can a consumer deal directly with the various producers of all the items he needs. Clearly there is a need for someone to sort out from a heterogeneous supply of goods and accumulate an assortment of items attractive to consumers.[2] This process of concentrating, equalizing and dispersing is performed by middlemen of various types.

The process is guided by the Principle of Minimum Total Transactions, the Principle of Massed Reserves, and the Principle of Proximity.[3] A slightly broader view of generally the same process is achieved by discussing the "utility" of items. A salable item must have four kinds of utility to the buyer: (1) *form utility* is created when materials are shaped into products; (2) *time utility* is created by storing the product until the consumer needs it; (3) *place utility* is created by transporting the product to the place where the consumer needs it; and (4) *possession utility* is created by providing a mechanism for exchanging possession and title fo the item. Manufacturing is generally regarded as creating form utility, and middlemen (and marketing in general) are regarded as adding time, place, and possission utility.

Thus, the distributor or middleman must match a supply of goods that is heterogeneous in terms of time, location, and quantity with a demand that is equally heterogeneous. This matching is accomplished by performing specific functions as described in a following section.

*Sorting Stolen Property*

The matching of supply with demand in the case of stolen property would seem to be an especially difficult task, since supply and demand are so heterogeneous. Supply assortments range from truckloads of surgical brassieres to saw logs to guns to diesel engines to liquor and a variety of other products. Consumer types include other thieves, suspicious businessmen, and unsuspecting consumers, among others.

The Marketing Concept[(4)] states that marketing is most efficient when the demand is calculated first and a supply created to match the demand. This generally is going to be difficult in the case of stolen property, although we find many instances where specific goods are stolen to match a previously determined demand.

Marketing theory also indicates that a fence would sort out, from a variety of stolen goods available, a selection of goods attractive to the market segment he serves. Thus, a given fence would be under extreme pressure to specialize according to types of product and perhaps also according to types of consumer.

The theory does support conclusively the evidence that there are indeed middlemen involved in the distribution of stolen goods. The mismatch between aggregate supply and aggregate demand is simply too great to be equalized by thieves themselves. It is the fencing activity which adds time, place and possession utility to stolen goods held by the thief -- goods that are unsalable without having these utilities.

## TRANSACTION AND EXCHANGE

### *The Theory of Transaction and Exchange*

The whole marketing function derives from a need to exchange surpluses of a commodity. The transaction, the act of exchange of ownership and/or possession of goods, is the basic unit of activity in marketing. Prior to the exchange, both buyer and seller are unsatisfied; the seller wants cash rather than the goods he has, and the buyer wants goods rather than the cash he has. The transaction and exchange remedies the situation for both parties. Depending upon the relative dissatisfaction prior to the transaction, there is a balance of trading power between the two parties.

Included in the transaction are elements of bargaining (about price, quantities, delivery and so forth) which can be either routinized by prepricing, prepackaging and so forth, or the elements can be determined by negotiation between the parties. To the extent that the negotiation elements are inconvenient to either party, a barrier is created which hampers the transaction.

The simplest transaction in a non-barter system of exchange is one in which goods and money are exchanged directly at arm's length risk. They range upward in degree of complexity with concurrent increases in risk, cost, and time, to ones involving promises to pay and deliver at distant points or at future times. All parties in a transaction bear some degree of risk.

The transaction function may be highly centralized or decentralized. In the highly centralized transaction, decisions on handling, storage, pricing and so forth are controlled by one individual or institution. In this case, one would expect a short channel of distribution and few middlemen. In a decentralized transaction, more latitude is given to other decision makers, and we would expect to find a longer channel of distribution and many middlemen.

*Transactions Involving Stolen Goods*

We find a variety of transaction-types involving stolen goods, ranging from rather routine to rather complex, and involving various degrees of risk and trust on the part of the buyer and the seller. A most important consideration in the transaction between a thief and "his" fence is that of risk. In turn, this requires an inordinate amount of trust between the parties -- a trust maintained in part by the unwritten "code of silence" which prevails in this subculture. In our own interviews and in ones reported by others, there is a tendency for a thief to refer to "my fence" or "our fence" in a rather possessive way, indicating that for a professional thief one of his most important business assets is a ready contact with a fence. There is also an outstanding reluctance among the thieves to disclose any information about the fence; even those thieves willing to disclose embarrassing personal information and information about crimes they had committed without detection would not reveal information about fences.

In a legitimate business the mechanical elements of the transaction are usually minimized and routinized to make the actual transaction as convenient as possible. However, an illegal transaction is typically surrounded by awkwardness, and the time, place, and other physical mechanics of the transaction lead to much inconvenience for both parties. To the extent that the transaction can be made more convenient, both parties benefit. One way to make it more convenient is to use specialist middlemen, such as a fence.

The necessity of using a fence highlights three problems of transaction and exchange: location, types of products and motivation to exchange. First, sources of supply and demand must be located. Second, the types of products to be exchanged must be determined. Finally, even though the sources and types have been located, the buyer and seller must be motivated and willing to exchange. A rational consumer simply cannot believe that a transaction involving stolen property is a very risk-free purchase, and it certainly is not a convenient transaction. These two elements alone severely limit the market for stolen goods, both in quantity and in the type of buyer. The motives and preferences of the parties are paramount considerations to an effective exchange, and are discussed in a later section.

There are two very distinctively different kinds of transactions in which stolen goods are exchanged between thieves, fences, legitimate dealers, and consumers. The distinction is made on the basis of the seller's effort to conceal the fact that the goods are stolen.

(1) In some cases, no effort is made to conceal the fact that the goods are stolen. It is most likely that this would be a rather simplified type of transaction which could occur at most any time or place with precautions to preclude detection by law enforcement officials. Both buyer and seller are taking risks, since both are subject to prosecution. However, with both parties trying to camouflage the exchange, there is much difficulty in detecting the exchange.

(2) In other cases, some effort is made to legitimize the transaction. The seller must convince the buyer that the goods are legitimate in order for the prospect to be a potential buyer. In this case, the seller is taking risk of conviction. The buyer is not

willing to take the risk. If he knows that the goods are stolen, he is not willing to buy, and may even report the attempt to sell. For instance, a legitimate art dealer reported a thief's attempt to sell art work and the thief was arrested and convicted. Since the seller must make an effort to disguise the exchangê, both to convince the buyer to buy and to convince the buyer not to report the exchange, there may be a tendency for the selling job to be done by a selling specialist -- a fence or some type who has a legitimate cover or front. However, there were several reports of cases where the thief did the legitimizing and selling himself, as in the case of selling stolen silver goods to a second hand jeweler or as in the case of disposing of goods through a pawnshop.

The most complicated exchange reported to us was a case in which the buyer bought (knowingly) a television set in a bar, without seeing the set beforehand. He paid the cash price and gave his car keys to the bartender who would have someone drive the car to another location, load the set, and return it to the bar. Thus, the buyer gave up cash and his car, trusting that the car would be returned with the right kind of goods. Surely, this type of exchange demands an inordinate amount of mutual trust.

## THE CONSUMER

### *Consumer Behavior: Buying Motives and Buying Habits*

Characteristics of consumer motives and behavior are a very critical element in marketing. A detailed consumer analysis is not within the scope of this study since the topic is really large enough to support its own research project. As in legitimate marketing theory, however, it is impractical to consider the market for stolen goods without also considering the preferences and characteristics of the consumer. Classification schemes that distinguish between the several types of consumers can be categorized generally into buying motives and buying habits.

Buying motives are the reasons a person decides to buy a certain brand or to buy at a certain outlet. Motives for buying a product may be inherent, such as a biological drive for food, or learned from time and experience in the marketplace. Motives also may be either *rational* (decision made strictly on the basis of price or functionality of the product) or *emotional* (to satisy prestige, status, maturity, or other psychological or social needs). A consumer's belief that he is getting a "bargain" is a strong buying motive, and provides part of the explanation for the market in stolen goods.

Buying habits are the patterns of behavior exhibited in the market prior to and during the transaction. The state of the buyer at the time of contact with the proposed purchase influences the search behavior of the buyer. Thus, a buyer may be in one of the following categories relative to the purchase of stolen goods: *unaware* that they are available; *aware* that they are available; *interested* in buying some; *intending* to buy stolen goods; or a *buyer* of stolen goods. In much the same way we can classify buyers of stolen goods into several usage classes ranging from *non-user* to *heavy user*.

Consumers can also be classified on the basis of their buying behavior. The way people buy a given product has been categorized into the following six types:(5)

1. A habit determined group of loyal consumers who tend to be satisfied with the product or brand last purchased.

2. A cognitive group of consumers who are sensitive to rational claims.
3. A price cognitive group of consumers who decide principally upon the basis of price or economy comparison.
4. An impulse group of consumers who buy on the basis of physical appeal.
5. A group of emotional reactors.
6. A group of new consumers of a given product who have not yet stabilized in their buying patterns.

As shown below, each of these categories is descriptive of a specific type of consumer of stolen goods.

*The Consumer of Stolen Goods*

Most consumers are probably not contacted as potential buyers by thieves or fences. If this is so, we expect that some regular users consume the major portion of stolen goods, that they are a market segment having a definable composition and that they are readily distinguishable from the remainder of the public. These factors create the possibility of making a consumer profile analysis -- a definition of the socio-economic boundaries of various kinds of users of stolen property. In turn, this would provide a great deal of information about the traffic in stolen goods.

For illustrative purposes, we can divide consumers of stolen goods into distinctively different categories. Investigation as well as prosecution varies with two important characteristics of the consumer: (1) if the buyer knows the goods are stolen, and (2) the frequency with which he buys stolen property.

We define an *unaware consumer* as one who buys stolen goods without knowing they are stolen. This could occur because he is buying in a supposedly legitimate outlet and has no reason to be suspicious. Even though he is buying products outside of regular channels, the thief or fence may make elaborate efforts to legitimize the exchange; i.e., a bartender sells a fur coat, claiming he had bought it for his girlfriend before they broke up. We define an *aware consumer* as one who knows full well, or reasonably should know, that the goods are stolen, and buys them anyway.

The frequency with which a person buys stolen property is an important characteristic as well, regardless of the state of awareness. We define a *light user* as one who rarely or perhaps only once buys stolen goods. A *heavy user* is a person who regularly buys stolen goods. It may be such a regular part of his behavior that he "checks around" about the availability of stolen goods prior to buying one in the legitimate channels. He expects to fill a substantial portion of his needs with stolen property.

Finer distinctions could be made between consumers by using the "medium" category as well, but little would be gained here by doing so. Thus, even with a simple classification, we arrive at four kinds of consumers: (1) an unaware light user, a person unknowingly buying stolen goods by buying in legitimate and marginal or second-hand stores; (2) an unaware heavy user, of which there are probably an insignificant number; (3) an aware light user, who may be buying for emotional motives; and (4) an aware heavy user, who is probably in an income and morality group where this is the necessary or accepted mode of behavior.

In the case of "aware" users, the consumer is likely to have buying habits that could be easily identified. For example, the consumer must be able to come into contact with a fence or a thief - a characteristic that is not necessarily widely held throughout the citizenry since many persons simply do not frequent bars nor have shady friends-of-a-friend. The consumer must have the full price in cash readily available since there is little or no use of credit. The consumer must be willing to assume the various kinds of risks involved -- especially the risk of detection and the risk that the product is unsatisfactory. The consumer must be someone who would prefer to buy the item this way rather than through conventional channels and he must be willing to tolerate the inconvenience of doing so.

Further, "aware" consumers would likely be distinctive in terms of their motives for buying stolen goods. Motives could range from money savings to the psychological thrill derived from "beating the system". However, the most powerful motive apparently is derived from the substantial price savings involved (price savings range from 25% to 90% reductions off regular retail). To gain this price saving the consumer must give up many conveniences that he could normally expect from the conventional channel of distribution; for instance, time, quantities, place, selection from an assortment, service, warranty, and others. These conveniences are a lot to give up for a price savings, and we expect that persons willing to do so are a rather unique and definable group.

Surely, a group of consumers with such unique buying habits and motives have demographic and socioeconomic characteristics that can be identified through research processes. Precise definitions of these characteristics would provide much usable information about market segments allowing one to build a hiearchy of markets according to the risk involved in selling to each. Much can be learned about a fence by studying the classes or groups which constitute his customers.

## FUNCTIONS OF THE MIDDLEMAN

### *Functions of Middlemen*

In the processes of concentrating, equalizing and dispersing goods, the literature generally reflects the fact that middlemen (and marketing in general) must perform eight separate and identifiable functions:[6]

1. Functions of Exchange: Buying, Selling
2. Functions of Physical Supply: Transportation, Storage
3. Facilitating Functions: Financing, Risk Taking, Market Information, Standardization

Any one of these functions may be more or less important than the others depending upon the situation but they must all be performed.

*The Selling Function.* Selling is "the personal or impersonal process of assisting and/or persuading a prospective customer to buy a commodity or a service or to act favorably upon an idea that has commercial significance to the seller.[7] The aim of the selling function is to accomplish transfer of ownership of a commodity. The selling function can be divided conceptually into five subsidiary functions:[8] (1) product planning and development; (2) the contactual functions required to make contact with a potential buyer; (3) demand creation activities of convincing the person to buy; (4) negotiation of the factors pertaining to the transaction; and (5) the contractual functions required to formalize the sale.

*The Buying Function.* Buying, which includes transfer of ownership (or possession in the case of stolen goods) is the marketing function of controlling or concentrating goods to facilitate sale, purchase, production, or use. Thus, purchases can be made for one of three objectives: buying for business use; buying for resale; and buying for ultimate consumption. Buying for business use may mean buying resources for use in production. Relative to buying for resale, the buying function can be divided into five subsidiary functions:[9] (1) planning a desired assortment of goods;

(2) contacting potential suppliers; (3) assembling a variety of goods; (4) negotiating details of the purchase; and (5) the contractual functions required to formalize the purchase. The buying and selling functions taken together add possession utility to the product.

*The Transportation Function.* The transportation function provides the physical transfer of goods from producer to user, including movement between the intermediaries required in the marketing channel. Basically, the transportation of goods adds place utility to the items. Differences in timing and location of markets require the transportation function to be performed.

*The Storage Function.* Storage involves holding goods for periods of time between the time they are produced and the time they are consumed. Storage tends to level out fluctuations and differences in quantities produced and demanded, and is a necessary function in matching supply and demand. Storage creates time utility in a product. The owner of goods in storage bears a risk that the goods may decline in market value during the storage period.

*The Financing Function.* "Market financing is that part of the general business function of providing and managing funds and credit which is directly related to the transactions involved in the flow of goods and services from producer to consumer or industrial user."[10] When goods are owned, capital is invested in them and the capital costs money. The financing function provides this capital.

*The Risk-Taking Function.* Risk typically is defined as a hazard of loss in which the probability of loss is known. Any time a middleman performs an activity relative to property, it costs him money, and he takes a risk that he can recover the money by selling the goods at a higher price than he paid for them. If the probability of risk is known the middleman can insure himself against loss.

*The Market Information and Research Function.* To the extent that marketing decisions are based on concrete facts, the marketing function will be performed more efficiently. Otherwise, decisions are made on the basis of guesses, and success will be a function of chance. Market research includes the gathering, recording and analyzing of all facts about problems relating to the transfer and sale of goods and services. Practically all areas of marketing are subject to scientific research processes, including market analysis, consumer research, advertising research, and others.

*The Standardization Function.* The standardization function determines the basic limits or grades in the form of product specifications to which manufacturered goods must conform, and the classes into which products may be sorted.[11] It also includes the activity of determining the appropriate quantities for package units.

In legitimate marketing, it costs money to perform each of these functions. Each function must be performed if goods are to be distributed. Each function is problematical to the marketer.

There is a tendency for middlemen to routinize the functions to gain economies of scale and economies of specialization. The more often a function is performed, the greater is the tendency to build an institutional framework for the activity. Some of the smaller functions, in fact, give rise to complex institutions for insurance and brokering. However, the more a function is institutionalized the more visible it becomes.

### *Functions of Middlemen for Stolen Goods*

In order to create equilibrium between supply and demand, all middleman functions are performed by someone at some point in the total transaction. The amount of time or sophistication present for each function may vary greatly with the type of good, its price, the amount of processing needed and other variables. Some activities may be accomplished by specialists, others by the thief himself.

*Selling of Stolen Goods.* Sales to various buyers differ in the amount of involvement of the seller. The quantity of items to be sold dictates in part the role of the middleman in selling. If there is a large quantity to be sold, the middleman or fence plays a larger part in arranging and facilitating the sale.

Direct selling is by far the dominant form of selling with respect to stolen property, although there may be a broker of some type who brings buyer and seller together. In some cases, the seller has the negotiating power, at other times not. Where supply is greater than demand, the seller usually makes the initial advance to begin the transaction.

*Buying of Stolen Goods.* The buying function is probably the most important function that the fence provides -- he is getting the goods off the hands of the thief. Statistics indicate that the number of buyers or fences of stolen goods is less than the number of sellers or thieves. The buying function of the fence is an illegal part of the transaction.

There may be reciprocal buying agreements where one fence agrees to buy a certain type of goods from another fence in return for the same agreement. In many instances of centralized marketing and in organized crime, the responsibility for buying decisions reposes in a group who decide what will be purchased and fenced. The individual buyer simply carries out his orders to buy and **fence** certain products.

*Transportation and Storage of Stolen Goods.* The transportation and storage functions can be most critical to the successful fencing of goods. The ability to move the goods from the thief to the next user is one of the prime responsibilities of the middleman.

Being able to obtain and provide goods at the right place and at the right time are the means by which time and place utility are created in goods that would be otherwise unsalable.

By token of their complexity and importance, the transportation and storage functions would seem to be among the most vulnerable links in the fencing operation.

*Financing of Stolen Goods.* The fence provides a major source of financing for the thief. The fence almost always has cash available and usually pays the thief directly and immediately in cash -- a necessary requirement for addicts and criminals in need of bail. As a middleman, the fence is in a position to turn the goods for cash and consequently is a major financer. This is true of second-hand dealers and pawnbrokers as well as the full-time fence.

A socio-economic analysis of individuals or types of businesses able to pay cash might yield valuable information as to the identity and operations of fences.

*Risk-Taking in Stolen Goods.* The thief faces one major type of risk -- the risk of detection during and after the theft. The fence faces two major types of risks -- the risk of detection while performing any one of the middleman functions *and* a significant economic risk. The latter risk arises because he has committed resources for goods and he may not be able to sell them at a profit. The fence is better able than the thief to protect himself against the risk of detection by means of alibis, covers and fronts, but he is generally less able to protect himself against economic risk. However, extortion, threats and other "insurance devices" associated with organized crime would provide some protection.

The fence faces risk in all of the middleman functions such as deterioration or obsolescence during storage or transportation, decrease in retail price of the goods in legitimate channels, and poor intelligence or market information.

*Market Research for Stolen Goods.* The dominant form of market information is apparently word-of-mouth communications between consumers, fences, information-brokers (e.g., bartenders) and thieves. We found no evidence of sophisticated data gathering and analysis similar to the very effective techniques used by legitimate businessmen. It is likely that syndicated crime does use such techniques on large volume transactions. When more thieves and fences begin using market research and intelligence gathering techniques similar to business and law enforcement agencies, we can expect increased traffic in stolen goods because these techniques are the first signs of market orientation.

*The Standardization Function for Stolen Goods.* Because thieves and fences deal mostly in goods already manufactured and packaged, the standardization function is not as important as others. However, in the case of cargo thefts of industrial or semi-processed goods, the standardization function takes on added importance because the fence performs some of the grading and packaging.

In summary, it is reasonable to expect that each of the middleman functions must be performed to a greater or lesser extent if stolen goods are to be distributed. Further, one cannot expect them to be less problematical for the thief or fence than they are for the legitimate dealer. We find evidence that specialists do exist in the channel of distribution for stolen goods. Their primary function is to solve the problems of distribution -- e.g., persons who provide contacts between sellers and buyers for a "cut" or fee. Other examples of middleman activities are examined in the following sections on marketing management and channels of distribution.

## MARKETING MANAGEMENT

Marketing management is the term used to describe the process of choosing a marketing strategy and a marketing mix. In visualizing the total activity of a marketing institution, it is widely held that the firm must create a total program of integrated marketing management decisions in the five major areas of channels of distribution, price, promotion, product, and market segmentation.

### *The Marketing Mix Concept*

This "mix" of marketing management decisions must fit a predetermined and well-defined market segment. The target market segment is a set of potential customers, homogeneous in the sense that they share a common need for, ability to buy, and willingness to buy the product being sold. A marketer will build a different marketing mix for each of the different market segments he serves in order to match the habits and motives of the market.

In legitimate business some production activities impose restrictions on the way the marketing function is implemented. The same situation holds true for the distribution of stolen goods. There are some problems involved in the theft of goods which dictate that the thief use certain marketing strategies in disposing of his stolen goods. Two of these "production" problems seem most critical in the case of fencing.

First, it is important for the thief to "get off the goods" as soon as possible. He is under great pressure to transport the goods from the site of the theft. Unlike a legitimate marketer, the thief usually cannot store the goods while waiting for better market conditions or for a better assortment. The minimization of risk by putting distance between the thief and the evidentiary goods is critical.

Second, it is usually important for the thief to get cash as soon as possible after the theft. A recurring point made by our sources was that they spend money as fast as they can get it and that they were always under real or imagined (often a desperate) pressure to get more cash. All sources stated that they would not release goods to an ultimate consumer without cash on the spot, although they may sell on very short-term credit (a few hours at the most) to a fence.

Otherwise, the thief and the fence have a good deal of flexibility in selecting a marketing strategy. In some ways, such as having low cost of goods sold and freedom from legal constraints, they have more freedom than legitimate businessmen. In other ways, such as concern about the threat of detection, they have less flexibility in their marketing behavior.

## CHANNEL OF DISTRIBUTION

### *Definition*

The channel of distribution is traditionally defined as "...the route taken by the title to the goods as they move from the producer to the ultimate consumer..."(12) This definition is obviously not usable for our purpose since the title to the goods is separated from the possession of the goods by the thief. Thus, the definition is altered to mean the path taken by *possession* of the goods between the producer (the thief who produces stolen goods) and the consumer (the person ultimately consuming the goods), since possession supplants ownership in the case of stolen property.

The channel is composed of a series of middlemen whose functions are routinized to the extent that their activities are repeatable. The channel has a structure, length, and process, each of which changes with type of product, type of customer, and with other variables. Structure is the relationship between the middlemen. Length refers to the number of steps involved in the distribution. The process includes the various functions performed by middlemen as detailed earlier.

### *Channels of Distribution For Stolen Consumer Goods*

We distinguish between specific channels of distribution for stolen goods on the basis of two key factors: consumer knowledge and type of product. First, a distinctive channel will be used if the consumer knows or reasonably should know that the products are stolen and that the exchange is illegal. A different channel will be used if the thief or fence must make some effort to legitimize the transaction. The second distinction is based on the type of product -- whether the goods are ready for consumption (the consumer market) or whether they must be substantially converted prior to final consumption (the industrial market).

Consider first the variety of channels possible for consumer goods. The channel structure, length, and process vary with consumer knowledge of the fact that the property is stolen.

*Consumer Knows the Goods are Stolen.* Here none of the parties are concerned with trying to disguise the fact that the transaction is illegal. The only difference between channels in this case is in terms of the number of middlemen invloved.

1. Thief (by direct sale) --- consumer. The thief makes no effort to legitimize the transaction. He does not have the problem of matching a very heterogenous supply with heterogeneous demand. He can solve this problem in part by getting an order for a specific product and then stealing it, a practice very much in line with the Marketing Concept described earlier. We would not expect this to be a very institutionalized or formalized operation. The transaction amounts to a cash-and-carry discount sale. The thief himself must perform each of the functions of a middleman.

2. Thief --- fence -- consumer. This channel structure would be used when the thief, for any of a number of reasons, cannot perform one or more of the functions of a middleman and must involve another person. Fences of the type used in this channel are apparently often bartenders and persons (such as prostitutes and others) who frequent bars. The bar is a good contact point because it provides contact with the most likely market segment. The fence may take possession of the goods and derive his profit from the sale. He may also act merely as a broker, bringing the buyer and seller together. When the fence takes possession of the goods, he is actually performing most of the functions of a middleman.

*Consumer Does Not Know the Goods are Stolen.* Somewhere in the channel an effort is made to legitimize the transaction by disguising the fact that the property is stolen. The legitimizing transaction is marked below by an arrow (→) in the following examples. Again, differences in channels involve differences in the number and type of middlemen involved in the flow.

1. Thief (by direct sale) → Consumer. In dealing directly with an unsuspecting customer, the thief must take steps of some kind to legitimize the transaction by giving an aura of legality, which may be difficult for many thieves. His price received is high, since there are no middlemen. His costs may also be high since he must perform all the functions of a middleman in addition to any costs involved in legitimizing the transaction.

2. Thief --- fence → consumer. In these cases, the thief himself either cannot perform one or more of the functions of a middleman, or cannot effectively legitimize the transaction. This may be the case where the volume of goods is so great that the thief cannot handle them and thus turns to a fence for the various middleman functions. The price received by the thief is lower, since the price to the consumer must be high enough to allow a margin for the fence. The fence may also place an order with the thief to provide specific items to match the market segment the fence has arranged. An important case of this type is where the fence operates a cover or front institution of some kind that provides an aura of legality to the unsuspecting consumer.
3. Thief → legitimate wholesale or retail outlet --- consumer. Truly legitimate outlets are hesitant to buy from irregular, non-institutionalized sources of supply. Thus it is usually

difficult for the thief to legitimize this kind of transaction, since he does not have an institutional base from which to work. This would seem especially true in sales to those wholesalers who typically buy direct from manufacturers. However, a thief of large cargo shipments may be able to build a cover story adequate to allow him to sell a shipment of goods, perhaps by posing as a manufacturer's representative. Many legitimate dealers do buy from non-institutionalized suppliers and some, such as pawn shops and dealers in antiques, stamps, coins, second-hand goods, silver and guns, must buy regularly from anyone walking into their store with even a weak attempt to legitimize the sale.

4. Thief --- fence → legitimate dealer --- consumer.
   When the thief cannot legitimize the transaction or when he cannot perform some function required for distribution, he must utilize a middleman. Again, this may be due to a high volume of goods involved as might happen from a cargo theft. Frequently, in cases of this type, the fence is someone who does have an institutional front or cover to legitimize the transaction with the legitimate dealer. Again, the thief's price must be low enough to allow for the margin required by the fence.

*Channels of Distribution for Stolen Industrial Goods*

Consider now the channels of distribution for industrial goods. These are products which are stolen and must be substantially converted before they are consumed. The goods which are stolen amount to supplies purchased by another company and which are then converted into consumer products, or are items used in the conversion process. In almost every case, there is a legitimizing transaction (as shown by the arrow) somewhere within the channel before the consumer.

1. Thief ⟶ legitimate supplier --- producer --- consumer.
   In this instance, we assume that the supplier is not aware that the goods are stolen and that the thief must make some effort to legitimize the transaction. This channel structure includes cases where a thief sells saw logs to a legitimate sawmill which converts them into lumber, and where a thief sells stolen cattle to a legitimate slaughter house. In cases where the legitimate supplier must buy from a large number of individuals, it may be fairly simple for the thief to legitimize the transaction.
2. Thief --- fence-like supplier ⟶ producer --- consumer.
   In some cases, the thief must utilize a fence who has an institutionalized contact with the producer due to the nature of the product and the way that supplies normally reach the producer. This is so in the case of stolen copper wire and for mercury stolen from gas meters. Once again, the price to the thief is lower because the fence must be allowed a margin. The fence simply merges the stolen goods in with a larger supply of legitimate goods.
3. Thief --- fence ⟶ supplier --- producer --- consumer.
   In some cases, the stolen goods do not

have to be converted into a new form but are useful only in an industrial setting. An example of this kind of product is the cargo of diesel industrial engines acquired in a truck hijacking. It is highly unlikely that an independent thief would have the ability to dispose of the products himself and would have to use a fence who had a legitimate cover.

It is difficult to determine the relative volume of stolen goods moving through each of the various channels. The wide variety of middlemen operating in the legitimate channels -- including rack jobbers, drop shippers, manufacturer's agents, brokers, commission men, truck jobbers, among others -- make it easy for a fence to assume a cover or a front for legitimizing sales. Blocking strategies and investigation models affecting all channels are suggested in Chapter 4.

## PRICE

### *Price Theory and Practice*

The price asked by a seller depends primarily on three related factors:

1. *Market demand*. Generally demand for the item will increase as price for the item decreases, as seen earlier.
2. *Cost*. Profitable sales dictate that the selling price must be greater than the cost of producing the item. However, it is generally held that cost determines profit rather than price.
3. *Competition*. As more persons try to sell similar items, the price will generally drop due to the increased supply.

The seller must balance each of these factors, although he may not have complete information about each of them, in arriving at a price which will be satisfactory to his market segment and to his profitability.

If one seller's price is higher than that of a competitor, he must offer some type of additional inducement to overcome the disadvantage. Common kinds of non-price competition are premiums such as trading stamps, services such as delivery or credit, and imputed quality differences created by promotion. As one seller's costs are lower, he can lower his price and increase demand for his output. Again, this seems to be a major factor in the continued traffic in stolen goods since thieves and fences are somewhat limited in the kinds of non-price competition they can mount against legitimate sellers.

There are a variety of objectives open to a seller, as well as strategies for achieving the objectives, by altering his price. Perhaps the first choice to be made is between a pre-priced, non-negotiable level (as is typically found in a supermarket), and a negotiated price to be determined by the bargaining power of each customer (such as often happens on a used car lot).

There are several objectives to be achieved by pricing:

1. Specified rates of return on investment or profit maximization.
2. Price stabilization.
3. Market share.
4. Competitive considerations.
5. Minimization of loss.

To accomplish these objectives, the marketer may adopt one or more of the following strategies for pricing stolen property:

1. Traditional pricing, where the thief customarily receives, for example, one-third of the retail value of the items fenced.

2. Discount pricing, where a fence sets his price to the public at "20% below retail", for example.
3. What-the-market-will-bear pricing, where the thief and fence agree on a price as a result of the balance between negotiating power.
4. Cost-plus formula pricing, in which the fence adds a fixed mark-up to the price he paid to the thief.

A widely regarded pricing procedure is the one provided by Oxenfeldt:[13]

1. Select a market target
2. Choose a brand image
3. Compose a marketing mix
4. Select a price policy
5. Determine a price strategy
6. Arrive at a specific price

A host of other problems face the marketer in arriving at a price which will allow him to compete effectively. The problems are of major significance since price is the most obvious difference between sellers in many cases.

*Pricing of Stolen Goods*

Again, price is a function of cost, demand, and competition. The total monetary cost of stolen goods sold is extremely low -- so low, in fact, that it is not really a price determinant. A major non-monetary cost of producing stolen goods is the amount of time spent in confinement if the thief is caught. Only one source, a thief who had spent many years in jail and who now has apparently gone straight, mentioned this as a "cost of doing business" and decided that it was too high. Other sources stated that the probability of having to pay this cost was so low that it really was not worth consideration.

Thieves and fences have the same problem in reading demand that a legitimate seller has. They can only estimate the relationship between price and quantity demanded, or use a trial and error method for determining demand.

Price competition among thieves is probably not too strong with respect to a given product. The major competitors are the legitimate dealers in the product.

Thus, the thief and fence are not able effectively to use cost, demand and competition in setting price. However, the thief and fence do have a very effective base upon which to arrive at the price for an item. Their pricing base is simply the regular retail price in legitimate outlets. The price received by the thief will probably vary around the base price with respect to two factors: (1) the efforts made to legitimize the transaction; and (2) the involvement of a fence in the channel.

Consider first the case where there is no effort made to legitimize the transaction -- both when a fence is used and when a fence is not used.

1. Direct sale from thief to an aware consumer. If the thief asks a price that is too low, he loses the opportunity for additional profit on the sale. If the price is too high, he loses some of the differential advantage of selling stolen goods, and must overcome this with an additional selling effort or with some form of non-price competition that is difficult for him to provide.

2. Sales through a fence. The price the thief gets from a fence must be low enough so that the fence can cover the cost of services he provides. These services are of two major kinds. First, since the fence takes some of the risk from the thief, there must be an additional cost to the fence. Secondly, the fence provides some real middleman services to both the thief and the

consumer. All of these services are costs to the fence and must be covered by the margin between what he pays the thief and what he gets from the consumer. For instance, the fence pays immediately and in cash. He typically has to store the goods in some way before they are sold to the consumer. In some cases he has to reform or grade the items, such as resetting diamonds or repairing tape decks damaged during the theft. Thus, the thief gets a lower price when he deals with the fence, but he gets additional benefits and services to compensate for it.

In the case where an effort is made somewhere within the channel to legitimize the transaction the pricing problem is more difficult.

1. Direct sale to consumer. In a direct sale to the consumer, the thief cannot ask a price that is too low for it would be an indication that the transaction is not legitimate. If the price is too high, the thief comes into direct competition with all the legitimate dealers handling the same product. Thus, the thief loses a differential advantage because he does not offer the services and conveniences typically offered by the legitimate dealer.

2. Sales through a fence. If the thief deals with a fence, the job of legitimizing the transaction falls on the fence. The thief is not under pressure to ask a high price to disguise the fact that the goods are stolen. By lowering his price the thief sustains an opportunity cost, but he obtains the necessary middleman services of a fence. The fence, by means of his

cover or front, can then ask a price that is below the regular retail price. The bargaining power relative to price also depends upon which individual takes the initiative in the transaction -- if a fence asks a thief to bring in a particular good, the thief has price bargaining power. If the thief tries to sell to a fence, the fence has price bargaining power.

In summary, the thief faces a dilemma in that his price may be too high or too low. However, the thief does have a ready reference in the regular retail price. The pricing objective of the thief is simply to arrive at a price that will move the goods and provide cash.

## PROMOTION

### *Promotion Concepts*

The objective of a promotional program is to stimulate demand for an item. The sequential problem faced by the seller is to create attention, interest, desire, and conviction on the part of the potential buyer to make an exchange with the seller. To achieve this objective, a promotional mix is created which may include advertising, personal selling, sales promotion, and other promitional tools.

The promotional program offered is thought by many to be closely related to the channel of distribution used. For instance, a long channel of distribution (one including many middlemen) typically also provides distribution over a wide geographical area and this requires a "broadcast" type of promotion provided by newspapers, magazines, radio and TV.[14] A short channel (the shortest is direct selling between producer and consumer) would best be served by the "closed circuit" promotion found in face-to-face contact between buyer and seller. The most effective promotion (and the most expensive) is that of a salesman in face-to-face contact with the potential buyer.

A similar model distinguishes between "push" and "pull" advertising. A "pull" strategy is one in which there is extensive advertising to the consumer who, it is hoped, will pressure retailers to stock the item. A "push" strategy is one in which the producer convinces the wholesalers and retailers to stock an item thereby providing exposure in the market.

A major problem in promotion is that of how to contact potential buyers. In general, it costs money to make a contact with anyone, and money spent on contact persons who are not really potential buyers is wasted circulation of advertising.

*Promotion of Stolen Goods*

Of all the parts of the marketing mix involving stolen goods, promotional aspects are the most difficult to describe because they are least prevalent. Again, we differentiate promotion strategies on the basis of the potential buyer's willingness to buy stolen property knowingly, and the thief's attempt to legitimize the transaction.

Consider first the situation where the buyer is willing to buy goods he knows are stolen. The most difficult part of the promotional problem faced by the thief or fence is attracting the attention of potential buyers. There is not a universally effective way of making contact or getting leads on potential buyers of stolen goods. Some sellers of stolen goods may make an overt attempt to contact potential buyers. About the most effective way of making contact is by word-of-mouth communications through friends and relatives. We often heard reference to a person bringing a quantity of goods (commonly a van-load of clothes) to a point in the Black community, and having friends spread the word through the neighborhood that a sale was being held. The goods would be exhausted within a few hours in one evening. Other sellers may wait for the consumer himself to make contact with the supplier of stolen goods by "asking around in bars".

Once the contact is made, interest in buying stolen goods is created by the low price of the item, desire may be accomplished by the thief's assurance of safety in making the transaction, and action is accomplished by arrangement for the exchange.

When the thief tries to legitimize the transaction because the buyer is not willing to buy goods that he knows are stolen, the thief is limited in the promotional techniques available because the method of promotion itself may be an indicator that the deal is illegal. One possibility for the use of broadcast types of promotion is the use of classified ads in a newspaper or the popular garage sale, although these methods require a "front" phone number and address. If the thief uses a fence who has a supposedly legitimate front, the fence has normal flexibility in selecting promotional programs.

## PRODUCT

### *Product Strategies*

A producer of goods has ample opportunity to design the product in such a way that it will be more easily salable. A variety of classification schemes are available to describe the differences between products which require a different type of marketing mix.

The most widely recognized classification shceme is to divide products into convenience, specialty, and shopping categories. A convenience good is a type of item that the consumer buys regularly, and one to which he is not willing to devote a great deal of time nor suffer inconvenience in making the transaction. He will not shop around, and will be willing to buy it at any time or at any outlet as his needs develop. Examples are cigarettes and bread. A shopping good is one for which the buyer is willing to compare prices and product features of several brands and in several outlets before he chooses a brand and outlet, as in the case of clothing. A speciality good is one in which the buyer knows exactly what he wants, and will go directly to the outlet that carries it, as in the case of a brand-loyal car buyer.

Another classification scheme is based on the motives for which the buyer makes the purchase. Thus, there are "prestige" products, bought to increase the prestige of the buyer among his reference groups, "anxiety" products bought to relieve some personal or social threat to the buyer, "maturity" products bought to make the buyer appear to be more mature, "hedonic" products which appeal to the senses, or "functional" products to which little social or psychological meaning has been attributed.(15)

Still another classification is on the basis of the pattern of behavior exhibited during the purchase itself. Thus, there are "habit" products bought as a regular part of any shopping trip, "impulse" products bought with no real consideration given by the buyer, or "cognitive" products in which the buyer carefully wieghs the pros and cons of the purchase.

In general, the seller will attempt to differentiate the product to give himself a competitive advantage in selling to his market segment. Manufacturers differentiate their product by changing the product design or package and then advertising those differences. Middlemen differentiate their product line by combining various products into an assortment that will be appealing to their market segment.

Legitimate marketers also must devise a product line strategy and create a product mix. A manufacturer may adopt full-line product strategy of offering a large number of variations of a product, or he could adopt a limited-line strategy of specializing in a few variations. A wholesaler or retailer must make the same decision about the degree of specialization of his product line.

*Product Strategies of Thieves and Fences*

The thief has nothing to do with the design of products since he almost always steals products that are already manufactured. A skilled thief or fence does make critical decisions about product lines, however, and can execute a product line strategy. This is accomplished when the thief is selective about what he steals and when the fence is selective about what he buys from thieves. In general, consumer goods most likely to be stolen for resale or fencing seem to have the following characteristics:

1. High value. This generates more cash per risky transaction for the thief or fence.
2. Low bulk and low perishability. These make it easier to transport the item from the point of theft, and provide flexibility in the storage and handling of the item.
3. Branded items. Items that are branded and those with a heavy promotion of the brand by legitimate sellers are much easier for the thief to sell.
4. Non-sized items. Items that are sized, such as shoes, complicate the problem of matching supply and demand.
5. Established and well known price. To show that the stolen goods are a real

bargain and to give the thief his only differential advantage, the regular retail price must be well known to potential buyers. The retail price is also used as a base price for negotiations between the thief and fence.

6. Three other features are of considerable importance, but perhaps not so critical as the ones above. Since the thief cannot offer a guarantee or warranty, the product should not be subject to extreme post-purchase dissonance. Further, risk increases with an increase in the traceability of the item. Finally, marketing opportunities increase substantially with an increase in the range of consumer types.

Consumer goods such as guns, gems, autos, television sets, and liquor all seem to have these characteristics in varying degrees. Industrial and commercial goods such as typewriters and adding machines are best examples of products having these characteristic features.

There are many exceptions to these characteristics. For example, brassieres, saw logs, shoes, pool cues, and meat have been stolen in volume and do not meet all of the important features. The exceptions suggest that perhaps one characteristic to be added to the list is "availability for theft".

In an economy of scarcity these characteristics would not necessarily hold true. Any item, regardless of perishability, bulk, or quality, that is scarce or rationed would be in strong demand. This would create a price inflated above production cost and would be subject to black market activity.

Even a heavy consumer of stolen goods cannot rely on a fence to supply items regularly nor with much convenience of purchase and would prefer to buy such items at the more convenient legitimate outlet. Thus, we would expect the general class of convenience goods to be fenced only when large quantities can be moved through legitimate channels. An exception, of course, is cigarettes, which are widely marketable. The fact that large quantities of convenience goods are occasionally fenced may give some clues to the channels of distribution for stolen goods.

At this point in time, there is limited marginal utility in classifying stolen goods on the basis of prestige, maturity, anxiety, or other types described previously. However, efforts to do so would probably yield additional blocking and investigative strategies.

## MARKET SEGMENTATION

### *The Concept of Market Segmentation*

"Market segmentation consists of taking the total, heterogeneous market for a product and dividing it into several submarkets or segments, each of which tends to be homogeneous in all significant aspects."(16) This strategy creates efficiency in the seller's attempts to reach his market informationally and physically.

A rational strategy for the seller is to design his total marketing mix (price, promotion, product, and channel of distribution) to fit the needs, motives, and buying habits of a specific group. In fact, the Marketing Concept states that the market segment be defined first and the marketing mix designed accordingly. If a seller deals continuously with the market segment, he can gain economies of specialization in production and distribution by using the experience gained from solving the same problems.

Substantial amounts of money are spent on defining the socio-economic boundaries of a seller's market segment. Efficient marketing research techniques are available for providing such descriptions.

*Market Segments for Stolen Goods*

To illustrate how a thief might segment his market, we consider the case of direct sales from thief to consumer. One method of segmenting, that based on the thief's acquaintance with the consumer, yields two segments requiring quite different marketing programs:

1. Friends and relatives. There may be some tendency for the thief to deal with friends and relatives if possible. Perhaps the most beneficial aspect of selling to this segment is the ease with which they can be contacted, and the concomitant decrease in risk. The problem of contacting potential buyers of stolen goods is one of the most difficult of the marketing problems faced by thieves, and it is clear that by dealing with friends or relatives there is a significant lessening of the promotion problem.
2. Cold-canvass of strangers. There is ample evidence that some thieves are successful in contacting strangers in bars or on the street and consummating the sale there. However, not all thieves have this option open to them -- especially if they are under a warrant for arrest and need to minimize visibility. Also, some thieves lack the personal skill to contact strangers. Disposal of goods by this fashion requires substantial time, since -- like fishing -- the thief must try several potential buyers before finding one willing and able to buy. Thus, there are substantial risks to the thief of detection and wasted effort. There is substantial risk to the buyer as well, since he often has to go to

another place to inspect or pick up the goods. If he does not have the cash on his person, he is not a prime potential buyer for the thief. If he does not have the cash, the buyer is subject to robbery.

A thief or fence might segment his market on the basis of risk of trading with consumers in the segment. For instance, a high risk market might be defined as one composed of consumers having high income and social status and who exhibit a code of behavior designed to protect that status. A low risk market segment might be defined in terms of low income and a moral value set that allows frequent contact with thieves and fences.

A thief may also segment his market on the basis of age, income or other characteristics of the consumer. The fence has other opportunities to segment his market more precisely in ways similar to those used by legitimate middlemen.

If a thief or fence concentrates on trading with a specific market segment -- perhaps an ethnic minority, or a certain income or age group, or persons working or living in a specific location, or persons unique in their drinking patterns -- his marketing activities must be tailored to fit that segment. Therefore, if one can define the market segment served by a thief or fence, we can learn a surprising amount about his marketing activities.

*Summary*

If a thief or a fence is marketing oriented, he can be expected to consider the concepts set forth in this chapter. As stated earlier, we believe that thieves and fences are becoming more marketing oriented; hence, the increasing traffic in stolen goods and the growing need for law enforcement officials to become marketing oriented. The thief or the fence weighs the advantages and disadvantages of each set of decision rules in determining a marketing mix and the strategies associated with each component.

Factors that a thief or fence may consider in arriving at a marketing program include their assessment of demand and supply, the variations in assortments of demand and supply, the complexity of the transaction, and exchange process itself, and consumer buying motives and habits.

Further, to conduct the marketing program, the thief or fence must perform the functions of the middleman which are buying, selling, transportation, storage, financing, risk-taking, market information and standardization.

Finally, in arriving at a marketing program, the thief or fence must make a series of management decisions in the areas of price, promotion, product line, channels of distribution and market segmentation.

The marketing of stolen property is a complex process. It is not something to be left to chance. Recurrent patterns of behavior associated with the traffic in stolen property are to be expected. Thus, marketing theory has promise as an instrument of law enforcement allowing an attack on orgainzed crime by attacking their marketing practices.

# CHAPTER III

## SELECTED INFORMATION SOURCES <u>RE</u> STOLEN PROPERTY

This chapter contains summaries of some of the interviews, surveys and other sources examined for this project. The interviews and cases reported here were selected to be representative of those which must be investigated more thoroughly in the future. The sources of information are from interviews with police and other law enforcement officials, from interviews with convicts and ex-convicts, and from printed and televised reports. In accordance with a promise to not give any indication about the identity of the respondents, no names, dates, or places are reported.

These sources do not represent all of the various types of traffic in stolen goods but are typical of some of the more common ones. Since this is an exploratory study we have no qualms about using second-hand reports and cases for illustration. While we are concerned with what thieves and fences do in fact, we are also concerned with what they could do and with what should do (according to theory) if they are reasonably rational and are guided by economic motives. For each case, a summary of the basic information is presented including a brief illustration of some of the marketing aspects involved.

*Source A*

The Chief Judge of a judicial district cited several examples of fencing operations -- the theft and fencing of brass bushings from railroad cars and the copper wiring from electric lines were two examples. The Judge was quite critical of the fact that the railroad companies do not press the prosecution of the receiver of these stolen goods. He urged that both railroads and other individuals prosecute the receiver, especially since the receivers were known. The Judge was quite emphatic that the emphasis of law enforcement should be directed toward fencing and receiving operations as well as theft of stolen goods.

> "It's much easier to catch a man who is receiving than a man who is burglarizing because the latter is one of millions, but as this burglar comes to a central point the stolen goods become concentrated so it should be easier to discover and uncover them, to uncover the fences, the receivers, the actual men who took (received) the goods.
>
> "A drive against all kinds of fencing for this is where the organization of crime is evident. The receivers of stolen goods are where organized crime is organized. These other 'punks' that go out and do their stealing are expendable. All the organized leaders want is the flow inward of stolen goods (from whatever source).
>
> "Without the commission of the receiving crime there is no profit in stealing."

An analogy can be made between traffic in stolen goods and narcotics. If emphasis is put on the pusher, then it makes it very difficult for addicts to be involved. Similarly, if the emphasis is put on the fencing operations, it makes it very difficult for the thief to operate effectively

*Source B*

An assistant district attorney for a large metropolitan area indicated that receiving cases are very hard to try and to prove in court. This individual believed it to be very difficult for stolen merchandise to get into the official channels such as the large, legitimate discount houses and wholesalers. This individual believed sales to smaller, marginal dealers to be more prevalent than any of the others. In his opinion, marginal dealers in certain so-called reputable businesses do take stolen goods -- sometimes knowingly. He did suggest that employees are responsible for a certain amount of pilfering and suggested that polygraph examination might be effective for cutting down on this type of pilferage.

*Source C*

The chief investigator for a district attorney's office suggested that a large amount of stolen clothing and office machines are fenced interstate. In fact, sometimes the goods are transported to foreign countries such as Mexico, while others with new identification plates or new serial numbers affixed to them are transported to other states. The fence, in this investigator's opinion, sometimes is paid as much as 70% of the legitimate market value. The percentage is high because he stores the goods until he accumulates a large enough volume to set up a shipment for out-of-town delivery. Transportation and processing (new serial or ID numbers) costs contribute to the high percentage. Out-of-town delivery is frequently made in a rental trailer full of stolen merchandise. This investigator believes that law enforcement agencies are very much hampered now because of the nature of search and seizure limitations on law enforcement officials; otherwise, they would stop some of the suspected interstate shipment by stopping the rental trailers and other suspected transportation vehicles.

Taverns are also an outlet for stolen goods, according to this investigator. Usually the fencing operation is a big one and fencing is not something engaged in by amateurs. Fences almost always get cash for their merchandise. The investigator made it clear that this type of outlet must know their customers very well and that they will not sell to just anybody because of their fear of unwittingly selling to law enforcement officials. The same is true for out-of-town fences. Since they must know their customers very well, there is a real need for brokers and other specialized middlemen. There is a high degree of organized crime involved in marketing stolen goods according to this source.

*Source D*

A US attorney described two instances where entire truckloads of merchandise were hijacked in the holding area of railroad terminals. The trailers came in via piggyback and the trailer and its cargo both were stolen. One truckload contained ski sweaters, another contained miscellaneous items including lawn mowers. In both cases, the thieves thought they were getting television sets. The lawnmowers and the ski sweaters were fenced through salvage companies and a "reputable" lawn mower rental shop.

The attorney described the fencing of a large truckload of stolen cigarettes and tobacco. They have been unable to prosecute this case because of a lack of identification of the cigarettes. The attorney also believed that salvage companies should be subject to a great deal of scrutiny.

*Source E*

A noted criminal lawyer stated that the channels of unlawful merchandise are well indicated. According to this source the pawnbrokers are a major participant in unloading stolen goods and may get $5 or $10 profit for a stolen $100 item.

According to this source, other channels of distribution include illegitimate or marginal dealers who at times deal exclusively in stolen goods and usually through interstate operations. The attorney suggested that if a carload of suits was stolen, that they would be scattered out -- not left in bulk for distribution. They would be farmed out to various retailers directly.

In some cases, automobiles are broken down into parts rather than sold as a unit. The network for automobile theft and distribution is well organized and there are organized crime payoffs or security setups involved. Burglars must have connections and many professional burglars have their market set up before they ever steal.

When asked which activities bore the most risk, the attorney answered that the actual act of theft was the riskiest, the delivery of the goods from the thief to the fence is the second riskiest, and finally the fencing operation is the least risky because the fence has more defenses and more alibis. The *delivery* of the goods to the fence is more risky than making a contact with a fence. So the fence is most vulnerable during the transportation phase of the operation.

*Source F*

According to one lawyer, who was convicted and served time for receiving stolen property, the majority of property stolen through shoplifting and burglary is stolen by non-professionals. There are some narcotics victims who finance 80% of their addiction through shoplifting. They also steal checks and currency from offices. The disposal of this material is made through street contacts and most of the disposal is at 15% to 20% of retail value. The average heroin addict needs between $150 and $250 a day in order to satisfy his needs for narcotics. At 15% to 25% of retail value, it would take approximately $1000 worth of stolen property per day to satisfy one addict's habit.

In the opinion of this learned ex-convict, office equipment is generally sold to small independent businessmen -- usually at about 10% of its retail value. Again, in the opinion of this individual, about 30% of the middle-class Black community in Denver now engages in knowingly receiving stolen property. Many of the thefts are accomplished through custodians of buildings or stores. For example, the night custodian will let somebody in to steal a number of suits. The thief will then take the merchandise to someone's house and word very quickly goes through the community that there are suits for sale as so and so's house at about 20% of the market value. Most of the clothing, then, ends up in the hands of individuals rather than going into stores, according to this source.

He was quite emphatic that the major outlet is not the pawnshops; that, as a matter of fact, the major outlet is through the ghetto community itself for clothing and similar items. However, there is some interstate shipments between Black communities.

Other ethnic groups are engaged in fencing and receiving particular types of goods. Many times a marginal dealer will have a stolen fur available for sale and will sell it to somebody at an ethnic community center. Or perhaps a hostess of an airline will go into a bar around an airport and get the story that, "Well, I bought this fur for a girlfriend and we broke up. Would you like to buy it?" In the case of the airline hostess, the purchase is usually made somewhat innocently. In the case of some other purchases like the one at the ethnic community center, the purchaser probably is not quite so innocent of the origin.

There are sophisticated receivers in the market for furs on the West Coast and in Las

Vegas. Contacts for fencing are probably made through persons in Las Vegas for a batch of furs worth perhaps a quarter of a million dollars. A whole load will then be taken to Las Vegas or Los Angeles for dispersal. This source suggested that it is not the better furriers who are the major targets of shoplifting thefts. First of all, the better furs are probably in a vault in the back of the store and if these were to be shown they would be brought into the showing room individually so that there would be very little opportunity for pilfering these furs. On the other hand, shoplifting at department stores runs quite high in the case of furs.

This source also suggested that employees are a major problem in pilfering goods and suggested the use of polygraph tests for employees. In his opinion, many thieves engage in crime because of a desperation or compulsion to return to an institution or penitentiary.

Finally, this source described the fencing operations as taking place in ways quite similar to the legitimate channels of business -- through middlemen and diversified retail outlets including the ghetto merchant and the direct face-to-face sale. In his opinion, very little was sold or fenced through pawnshops except perhaps, in the case of jewelry dealers where the jewelry was broken up and reset. He did not believe that bail bondsmen or lawyers were much involved in receiving stolen goods. Incidentally, this was the crime for which he was sent to the penitentiary and according to him, no one has dared get caught since he was convicted. Sometimes, the lawyer can get caught holding the goods not so much for purposes of resale - but simply as security for legal fees.

*Source G*

Another former convict and at one time a thief with a big operation in Denver breaks thievery down into four categories: Petty thieves addicts; shoplifters; and the professionals. The housewife who could afford to buy the item and the teenager who goes out after school to steal items fall into the petty thief category. The addicts, most of whom are armed, comprise another category. The shoplifter engages in the crime sometimes for personal use but frequently sells to a fence. Finally, there are the professionals who by definition make their full-time livings by shoplifting or burglary.

The fencing operation is more complex. According to this source, fences are very selective in the kinds of items they will take. Shoes, for example, are difficult to steal and fence because of various sizes and complications of selling. There is usually a middleman between the thief and the fence himself and that middleman usually gets a flat fee of $100 or upward depending on who he knows and what kinds of contacts he has. There is a chain reaction and a "take off" at each level of distribution. There are fencing specialists for various commodities. One individual deals in clothing and another deals in jewelry but they all know each other. If there is somebody who is trying to unload a package of jewelry, he can contact a person who normally deals in clothing and within a few hours be apprised of how to get rid of it through a jewelry fence. The seller of jewelry usually gets 10% to 15% of the retail value, according to this source.

Typically, the fence is the individual who receives the largest amount of money. The bargaining power relative to price frequently rests with the individual who is asked about the transaction -- if a fence asks a thief to bring a particular good, the thief has the bargaining power. If the thief tries to sell to a fence, the fence has the bargaining power.

In the distribution of jewelry, some recut and remounted gems do show up in pawnshops. In the distribution of furs, there is considerable inter state activity. But for other clothing -- particularly men's clothing - there are ample opportunities in the ghettos to sell merchandise that has been stolen in that geographical area as well as other cities.

*Source H*

In the case of professional thievery, the demand for a stolen good is almost always present before it is produced (stolen). One individual (presently an inmate in the state penitentiary) states that he had an agreement to supply 10 to 20 auto tape decks per week. He distributed these through a partner who had an uncle that would pay $5 for each deck. The uncle apparently had several other thieves supplying him with decks, including the partner. The convict had no idea about where they went except that he believed the uncle took them to Denver. The convict stole them all in a town near Denver. He operated at this rate for "several months". Since he was arrested during a burglary of a liquor store, police had no idea the convict was previously stealing tape decks on a regular basis.

In burglarizing homes, the convict apparently was very selective in the items taken - his specialty was guns (based somewhat on a personality quirk as well as on economic reasons). He related the experience of once having taken a large electric guitar amplifier and of how this was an unwarranted risk -- that it was too bulky to carry and difficult to fence. He stated that he could go into any town and within two or three days and with no previous contacts, locate a fence who would buy stolen guns. He would begin by asking around in bars.

According to this individual a professional fence deals in several kinds of goods. The thief preferred not to wait to fence the goods -- that is not to store the goods -- but he had to do so in order to meet the conditions and quantity requirements of his fence.

The very low price received by the thief may reflect several things. It may be evidence of a large supply of stolen tape decks. It may also indicate a long channel with several middlemen between the thief and the consumer. The multiple stages of the channel are also suggested by the fact that a number of stolen tape decks were supplied without connecting wires and mounting brackets. These would have to be provided by someone in the channel prior to sale to the consumer (especially if the consumer was unaware the goods were stolen).

The thief's product line consisted of items with concentrated value and ones having a reasonably well established market value. Risk to the thief occurred at several different points: (1) at the time of the theft; (2) at the time of first sale to the fence (the fence could have been an undercover agent or a tipster); and (3) during storage of the decks until delivery and during delivery.

*Source I*

This convict owned and operated a small auto repair shop doing a submarginal amount of legitimate business. In a way that he would not disclose, contact was made with a fence who arranged to have high school aged boys deliver stolen autos to the garage. The subject "repairman" would pay around $50 per car to the boys. He would immediately alter the car -- by painting it with primer paint -- and within one to three days the fence would come for the car, paying the subject anywhere from $100 to $400 for the work. The repairman also ground off serial and other identification numbers although he knew the old numbers could show up under an acid test and that other hidden numbers could give him away.

The convict would not disclose anything about the fence or even about the nature of the fence. In fact, he took sequential sentences rather than disclose this information to the police. He did say, however, that there was a possibility that the cars were being taken out of state for sale and that there was some Mafia connection.

This man was performing auxiliary functions in the channel -- that of risk bearing and some creation of form and time utility. He also provided an important break in contact and identification between the fence and the thief. He also reduced the overall risk of the activity by altering the product to reduce the chance of detection.

Subsequent to our interview, this man escaped and was able to contact a fence in Las Vegas where he had never been before and was able to do it rather quickly.

*Source J*

This individual was a convict who would steal silver during home burglaries -- usually at night. The silverware would be sold to legitimate dealers in used silver. The dealers resell and reprocess old silver. This thief would be well-dressed and unhurried in contacting the dealer under the pretext of settling an estate. Stolen goods were always taken to a different city for selling. (Police communications and notification were not good between cities.) The thief worked over a wide geographic region of the Midwest. Little time (a day or two at most) passed between burglary and selling. Perhaps the legitimate dealer would ask to hold the goods for appraisal or ask to be able to make a payment a few hours later. The subject did not object or show concern at this arrangement as part of his attempt to legitimize the transaction.

The price was established by the legitimate market for used silver. There is a very short channel based on direct selling. Other than the usual risk during the burglary, the main risk occurred to the thief while he tried to legitimize the transaction and while waiting for the appraisal. The thief was not willing to take a low price for goods so the buyer would not become suspicious.

The subject maintained that the vast majority (90% -- his estimate) of home burglaries were committed by professionals and semi-professionals. This somewhat contradicts Source F who maintained that most property is stolen by non-professionals. Undoubtedly, there is a middle ground of semi-professionals between the two extremes on which both of these sources and others could agree. This category would include the addict sustaining a habit.

*Source K*

One subject maintained that most of his education in thievery and fencing had come from intermittent terms in jails and penitentiaries. This "crime educated" subject estimated that 90% of theft related crimes are committed by those under 25 years of age, including those who are not caught and hence would not be reflected in criminal statistics. The sophisticated element of the transaction is fencing the goods. Generally, the complexities and risks rest with the fence rather than the thief. Hence, the thief usually gets only 20% to 25% of the regular retail price. For some readily marketable items (those requiring little modification such as gems), the thief may get as high as one third of the regular market value.

The professional thief knows where and at what price he is going to fence the goods before he ever steals them. Fencing outlets include vending companies and retail stores for cigarettes and related sundry items.

According to the subject, the fence provides the bulk of financing and storage functions since the thief usually sells the items immediately or soon after theft -- overnight at the longest. The fence may take the "hot goods" off the thief's hands and pay him later -- usually only a few hours later. The fence is often a legitimate businessman who maintains a token inventory of legitimate goods. Consequently, the fence may hold onto the goods for a fairly long period of time. With the stolen goods intermingled with legitimate goods, the fence has a good cover.

*Source L*

The most professional burglar and thief encountered during the study put priorities on the items to be stolen and fenced. Cash was always best -- if available; then, jewelry, coins, stamps, and some art. Never did this thief steal credit cards or other traceable items. Other sources stated that they stole goods because of a desire or motivation to possess different tangible items even for a short period of time. This source also suggested that the reason for the burglarizing of homes instead of stores was that "electronic devices scared off" burglars and that there was frequently a longer penal time involved for store theft than home burglaries.

He described himself as a professional jewel thief who also dealt in small items that he could carry on his person, thus not hindering his mobility. Television sets or other large items would slow down transportation and create storage problems for the goods. Because of lower risks and higher profitability in book-making, this source indicated that he would change his "profession" when released from the penitentiary.

The storage function was sometimes performed by the thief who kept some small diamonds and other gems to accompany larger stones when selling to individuals and marginal dealers. Usually very little time passed between the theft and fencing operation. The subject agreed with other interviewees that price was usually negotiated for jewelry and other specialty items. Rather, it was necessary that the thief know an individual or a marginal businessman who wanted the goods. This professional thief set his price (usually about 40% of retail for jewelry) rather than taking the price set by a fence.

*Selected Secondary Sources*

The proceedings of the Senate Small Business Committee, chaired by Senator Alan Bible, contain much valuable information on the serious matter of cargo and transportation thefts. Truck hijacking as well as shipping and air cargo thefts amount to one billion dollars a year, according to the committee staff.

The editors of the *Wall Street Journal* have compiled an anthology of articles on theft and other crimes in *CRIME AND BUSINESS*.[(17)] Included therein are some detailed descriptions of the infiltration of crime into business -- and of business into crime. Many of the examples cited expose some of the marketing practices used by thieves and fences.

Various other sources, such as the *Journal of Insurance*, the syndicated Scripps-Howard series on theft,[(18)] the CBS television series on thefts from shipping terminals and truck hijackings, provided additional background for the study. Almost daily, news items relating to thievery and fencing appear, and were also utilized.

*Summary*

The general economic awareness of thieves and fences provides an enviable reference point for many law enforcement officials. These criminals' working knowledge of the laws of supply and demand and the market structure permit them to carry on a significant amount of crime.

The reasons for specialty in the theft or fencing of a particular type of stolen good are varied. As noted earlier and by several sources, there are frequently psychological and social reasons for their preferences. More germain to this study, however, are the varied economic motives and reasons for specialty and structure in a particular product and market segment. There is a certain amount of naivete on the part of some administrative and law enforcement officials regarding these economic considerations.

One of the major difficulties in conducting our research arose from the non-avialability of individuals knowledgeable about fencing operations. Penitentiary inmates and law enforcement officials alike are familiar with the operations of thieves; very few, if any, really understand the methods and marketing practices of the fence. Consequently, the most cogent fact to come from our study of sources was that both research and action emphasis should be put on fencing operations in order to thwart thievery.

The willingness of the thief to bear risk during transactions in stolen goods suggests an entrepreneurship advocated in our society. The challenge now is to make law enforcement officials as aware of the dynamics of the market situation as the thieves are. Finally, the gullibility of the consumer is a major contributing factor to the continued traffic in stolen merchandise.

# CHAPTER IV

## CONCLUSIONS AND RECOMMENDATIONS

This chapter provides the major conclusions drawn as a result of the study. Most of the conclusions are in the form of recommended programs for additional research and action. Other observations and conclusions appear in the text where appropriate, especially in Chapter II.

### CONCLUSIONS

Marketing theory provides a fresh and effective foundation for studying the traffic in stolen property. It allows law enforcement agencies to visualize theft and fencing activities from much the same perspective as that used by thieves and fences.

Professional and organized thieves and fences face a formidable marketing task in general, and especially so in the case of large-scale cargo thefts. Because the marketing problem is so complex, the fence must make an overt effort to solve it. Once he does -- that is, once he becomes marketing oriented his behavior pattern becomes *predictable* by use of marketing theory and concepts.

Thus, by studying the question, "If a thief or fence were marketing oriented, what would he do?", police agencies are attacking the crimes of theft and fencing by attacking their logical marketing practices.

Without doubt, the most problematical area is that of the lack of readily available data, statistics, and information relating to the traffic in stolen property. This problem is caused largely by lack of budget, traditional use of statistics primarily for budgetary purposes, and other characteristics of law enforcement agencies. There seems to be a tendency for departments to record data more for the purposes of budget support and for public reporting rather than for any very sophisticated kind of operational or investigative purpose. For example, we have tried for the duration of the study to obtain data to complete a table similar to the one in Exhibit I, without results. In the business sector, critical basic information of this type would be widely available even in secondary sources of information. Data of the type described in Exhibit I compiled by time periods and geographical regions would permit departments to accomplish planning and investigation merely by looking at trends and comparisons at a fairly uncomplicated level. Further, there is a surprising lack of transfer of information between and even within many departments.

Police reporting forms themselves are often poorly structured and are often completed with errors and omissions. In one department, when an auto is stolen a loss value equal to the value of the car is reported. However, when the car is recovered stripped of parts, the recovery value given is the original value of the car, lowering the reported value of items stolen and inflating the recovery statistic. In a study of the theft of bicycles on a campus, 41% of the reports did not include the time of the theft, 26% of the reports did not include the day of the theft, and 12% did not indicate whether it was a man's or a woman's bike that was stolen.

Much of the problem with police reporting is understandable and is probably not correctible. Further, not all of the lack of information is due to inadequate police reporting.

The code of silence among thieves is especially powerful relative to fences or fencing activities. In addition, most professional fences keep the thief unaware of the fence's activities. Thus, there simply

EXHIBIT I. ESTIMATED DISPOSITION OF STOLEN PROPERTY -- IN PERCENT
(not including cash, checks, credit cards)

| A. Stolen Property that is NOT Recovered: | Clothing | Guns, Bikes, Sports Eq. | Appliances, TVs, Radios | Autos, Parts | Furs | Jewelry | All Other |
|---|---|---|---|---|---|---|---|
| 1. Resold by thief (as % of total category) | | | | | | | |
| a. person-to-person (Hey, buddy--want to buy a watch or gun?) | | | | | | | |
| b. to fence, who knows goods are stolen | | | | | | | |
| c. to legitimate dealer including pawnships | | | | | | | |
| 2. % used by thief | | | | | | | |
| 3. % given to family or friends of thief | | | | | | | |
| 4. % lost or abandoned by thief | | | | | | | |
| B. % Recovered | | | | | | | |
| TOTAL (by Category) | 100% | 100% | 100% | 100% | 100% | 100% | 100% |

are not very many fences in confinement or otherwise available for interview.

Another source of problems is the lack of continuity of operations by thieves and fences. Most institutionalization or routinization of their activities is necessarily done in ways that reduce visibility of the operation. This gives rise to a surprising variety of operations, making it difficult to draw generalizations and principles. A related factor contributing to this difficulty is the surprising variety of products stolen for distribution.

Still another source of problems is that thieves are not totally rational or sophisticated in business practices, even though they act in general as if they want to maximize profits rather than to satisfy psychological needs. A substantial number of arrests of thieves occur when the thieves are too drunk to be rational. A number of sources related that several of their biggest deals were made either in a state of drunkenness or as a stroke of luck.

## RECOMMENDATIONS

Two kinds of recommendations are provided. First, we recommend additional research be devoted to rounding out the application of marketing theory. Second, we suggest an action program consisting of marketing-based blocking strategies and investigatory models.

## SUGGESTED RESEARCH TOPICS

Listed below, not by any priority, are selected research questions. Answers to these and other questions will be needed if marketing analysis is to be fruitful in tracing the flow of stolen property, and if the blocking and investigatory strategies discussed later are to be fully implemented. Further, investigation of these and other questions will suggest additional strategies not yet conceived.

No attempt is made to suggest research approach or design, even though several techniques such as survey research, Delphi,[19] and other exploratory techniques seem particularly applicable to some of the questions. Most of the questions below are no more difficult to answer than the ones routinely answered by market research conducted for business organizations.

1. What are the socio-economic demographics of the aware, heavy consumers of stolen property?
2. What are the critical buying habits of the aware, heavy consumers of stolen goods?
3. What percent of stolen goods are ultimately sold through legitimate marketing outlets to unaware consumers?
4. What is the most effective way for a thief or fence to legitimize the sale of stolen property?
5. How does the channel of distribution vary with the characteristics of the stolen item?
6. How are market segments for stolen goods ranked according to risk and profitability?
7. What are the fence's considerations when deciding to specialize in a particular product?
8. How do thieves and fences arrive at a mutually agreeable price?
9. What factors are important to the fence in pricing his product to the consumer?
10. How can fences who have "legitimate" fronts or covers successfully merge stolen items into their stock without revealing their origin?

Further, business research methods similar to the marketing research methods suggested here can be applied to the study of personnel, management, accounting and other business dimensions of organized crime.

## A SUGGESTED ACTION PROGRAM

Listed below are selected strategies based on marketing and management concepts which appear to be useful in restricting the traffic in stolen property or for investigating specific cases dealing with stolen property. While some of the strategies could be implemented with the current state of knowledge, others will require additional research prior to their implementation. Some strategies suggested are in use by some law enforcement agencies now and are reported here because they illustrate the marketing dimension. Some are directed at the thief, some at the fence, and some at the consumer of stolen goods.

The strategies are presented solely to illustrate how law enforcement can be enriched by marketing concepts. Chapter II illustrates what a thief or fence could do if he were marketing oriented. This section illustrates what law enforcement agencies could do if they were marketing oriented.

### *Blocking Strategies*

Blocking strategies are actions taken by law enforcement agencies to make the traffic in stolen goods so expensive, time-consuming or risky that there would be a significant lessening of incentive to deal with stolen goods. Several basic principles and more specific marketing based blocking strategies are listed below.

The traffic in stolen goods is deterred to the extent that the channel of distribution can be lengthened. As the channel is lengthened, the price of stolen goods must be higher. As the price approaches the legitimate retail price, the fence loses his primary competitive advantage. Thus, any action that would cause more middlemen to be involved in distributing an item lowers the profitability of the traffic and thereby lowers the incentive to trade in stolen goods. Lengthening of the channel may increase the probability of detecting the traffic (due to more chance of error by the fence) although a step-by-step tracing of stolen goods would be more difficult.

Anything that can be done to increase the price of stolen goods would provide effective blocking of the traffic. Methods for increasing the price include jamming channels of communications, lengthening the channels of distribution, and restricting the traffic to low-margin items. These methods and others are discussed in other blocking strategies.

Traffic in stolen goods is deterred to the extent that the actual transaction can be made more inconvenient. The competitive advantage of a fence is his low price to the consumer who must accept inconvenience during the transaction. Thus, the fence's competitive advantage decreases as the transaction is made more inconvenient.

The ability to block the traffic in stolen goods increases as the supply of stolen goods becomes greater than demand. The fence must take more risks and become more marketing oriented if he deals in the buyer's market created by excess supply. A change in his marketing program makes him more vulnerable to efforts made toward blocking his marketing operation.

The classification of types of transactions would yield those to which high priorities should be assigned for further investigation. A study of transactions would also yield certain definable patterns of exchange. When one can define a pattern, he gains the ability to categorize and classify transactions. In turn, this allows him to isolate the type of transaction most susceptible to detection; for example, the ones most risky due to prolonged or repeated contact, or the ones most costly to the fence in terms of time or money. One could also determine the transaction type most vulnerable to deterrence; for example, the one which requires the most sophisticated efforts to legitimize.

The point at which a conviction for receiving is most likely is at the transaction just prior to the legitimizing effort, since both parties know the goods are stolen. The most difficult kind of transaction during the flow of goods is at that point where the thief or the fence makes an effort to legitimize the transaction, since he has two things to do at once -- make the sale and make it appear legal.

Effort can be most effectively directed toward reducing the volume of transactions with aware buyers by choking off supply or demand. This can be accomplished by making such transactions even more inconvenient. Since transactions with aware buyers are very easy to conduct in an open society, only marginal benefit can be gained from devoting extensive effort to transactions where both buyer and seller try to cover the exchange.

Public service advertising programs directed at consumers could be effective in blocking some traffic in stolen goods by reducing primary demand. Because an aware but light user of stolen goods is expected to be somewhat nervous about undertaking the transaction, an advertising theme playing on this anxiety by stressing the danger of muggings and fraud could be effective. Persons who are unaware that they are buying stolen goods might be influenced by an advertising program built on a theme such as, "Why buy outside of regular channels, since it is so inconvenient to do so?". The objective of these kinds of advertising programs is to limit the market potential of fences thus slowing the traffic by making it less profitable. Such a program would probably not be effective in influencing the aware, heavy user, although additional research might discover some motive that could be played on in reaching this group.

Law enforcement departments should determine the universal elements of buying habits exhibited by aware heavy users of stolen goods. Since there is little hope of deterring them by attacking their buying motives, information about who they are and about what, when, where, and how they buy could indicate effective means of blocking their transactions.

Licensing or registration of the various kinds of middlemen might provide an additional difficulty for a fence in his operations. Since they often pose as a representative of a legitimate institution when selling stolen goods to unaware wholesale or retail outlets, licensing would cause the fence to take an additional step in his marketing.

A careful monitoring by law enforcement agencies of the assortment of goods maintained by suspected thieves and fences in a market area would provide useful information about the market they serve, about the demand for stolen goods in the market and about the buying habits of their customers. Fences can be classified as being either specialized or generalized, allowing law enforcement agencies to tailor blocking strategies accordingly.

Law enforcement departments can destroy the integrity of the channels of communication that are so necessary to the traffic in stolen goods. Communications and promotion channels are very informal and subject to considerable noise and interference. Since promotion is so vital to distribution, the distribution can be partially blocked by making communications unreliable and inconvenient -- perhaps by "jamming" the channels with false information about the availability of stolen goods.

Better interdepartmental cooperation and exchange of information about suspected stolen items travelling out of a geographical market area into another jurisdiction would force the fence to take additional risky steps. Additional middlemen or storage would be required to overcome these increased risks.

The identification of goods with numbers and secret marks is most desirable. Businesses themselves would benefit from serialization or other identification because of efficiencies in inventory and stock control. Insurance companies, too, would be in a better position to assess and pay claims. In fact, insurance companies might require better identification or serialization as a condition of insurability. But the most important aspect of better identification is the deterrent effect on the potential thief. This deterrent effect emanates from the increased power of law enforcement officials to better identify and locate stolen property.

Pawnshops, while not the major outlet for stolen goods that some sources believe, are a major outlet for stolen gems and reset jewelry, and for small volume of other goods stolen by semi-professional and amateur thieves. This knowledge should alert law enforcement agencies to continue close surveillance of this outlet. The rationalization that pawnshops are a major outlet of other stolen goods should be investigated further. Large volumes of new TV sets, new clothing and furs, and various other high value items exclusive of jewelry, are probably not fenced through this outlet.

Means of identifying sources of materials available for sale in salvage yards and second-hand stores must be found. These outlets are ready-made and effective opportunities for fencing. A required waiting period prior to resale of goods would permit spot checks and close surveillance by police to determine true ownership. Auction houses, bazaars, flea markets, and garage sales should also be subject to spot checks, since they are also effective outlets for stolen goods.

The best blocking strategy is the prosecution and conviction of fences. Giving some thieves immunity for turning states' evidence may well be worth the public wrath incurred to identify, study, and prosecute fences.

*Investigatory Models*

An investigatory model is a systematic way of visualizing the diverse activities related to the traffic in stolen goods. An investigator is faced with sparse and seemingly disconnected observations. An investigatory model is designed to connect these observations. Thus, case evidence becomes more meaningful, and the investigator can predict the existence of activities and institutions before actual facts become avialable. This would allow investigators to short-cut the tortuous chain of obscure clues by indicating those activities which are most likely to occur with respect to a given crime. Several general principles of investigation and specific models and procedures are discussed below.

An investigator may classify stolen goods on the basis of their marketing characteristics -- allowing him to devote different amounts and kinds of energy to the different types of products and market segments. For example, a thief distributing a large quantity of convenience goods will almost surely have to use a fence who has contact with dealers that have high sales volume through multiple outlets. On the other hand, he could use personal contact selling with shopping or specialty goods.

Better incident and statistical reporting on the part of police and other law enforcement agencies would make the tracing of stolen property much easier. Reporting officers are frequently not descriptive nor specific in describing the kind of property stolen. The ability to investigate specific cases increases with both the precision of identification of the goods and with the precision with which field reports are completed.

The permanent identification of items permits easier tracing of the goods and also serves as a blocking action since it forces an additional step into the flow of stolen goods. Well identified items represent a direct risk to the thief and fence who must take steps of some kind to circumvent the identification.

Law enforcement agencies must increase their efforts to monitor the equilibrium between demand and supply of important types of stolen goods. Three questions should be answered continuously for each type of good. First, for a given time, product and area, does the thief or fence typically initiate the transaction? Second, is the price for the item increasing or decreasing? Third, are thieves or fences shifting from a more risky or less risky market segment? Answers to these questions would allow the investigator to determine the degree of equilibrium between supply and demand for each important kind of item. In turn, if supply is greater than demand the investigator can expect that perhaps the goods have been transported into the market area, and can endeavor to determine the supply area from which they have been shipped. If supply is substantially greater than demand, he would expect shipments out of the market area. If the answers indicated that supply is less than demand, the investigator can expect either increased thefts of the item, or shipments into the market area from other points.

Several specific operations now in use could be more effectively employed for continuous monitoring of supply and demand. These include Crime Check, pawnshop details, informants, undercover agents, and a more complete questioning of suspects and victims.

Communications between departments, including comparison of theft and recovery reports, would allow a more complete determination of areas which are suppliers and those which are markets for specific types of stolen goods at a given time. The investigation program would be substantially different if the investigator were looking for thieves than it would be if he were looking for a fence in a market area.

Increased patrol and surveillance of warehouse and other storage areas by both private and public security agencies may yield information on storage points and caches of stolen goods -- albeit that garages, barns and other locations outside of the industrial areas are major storage areas. Similarly, closer observations of transportation marshalling areas by both private and public agencies may give clues to the types of transportation mechanisms used in large cargo thefts.

Sophisticated statistical analyses of a department's theft and recovery reports, including a comparison between departments, would provide invaluable information about demand and supply equilibrium among other things. Many ratios and computer plots of theft and recovery data can be calculated continuously by the computers available for use by departments of all sizes.

The most effective investigatory strategy available to law enforcement agencies is that of incorporating the study of marketing concepts and practices into the training of investigators. Investigators must be more aware of marketing theory than are the thieves and fences.

Increased investigation and law enforcement efforts in the aforementioned areas may require assignment of increased manpower to fencing operations. On the other hand, if these investigations are fruitful (as we believe they can be) less manpower will be required on theft and related investigations. If the demand for stolen goods is reduced by disrupting or blocking the fences, the production or theft of stolen goods will necessarily also be reduced.

# NOTES

## CHAPTER I

(1) Committee on Definitions, *MARKETING DEFINITIONS: A GLOSSARY OF MARKETING TERMS*.
(2) Stanton, *FUNDAMENTALS OF MARKETING*, p.5.
(3) Fisk, *MARKETING SYSTEMS: AN INTRODUCTORY ANALYSIS*, p. 10.
(4) Bartels, *THE DEVELOPMENT OF MARKETING THOUGHT*.
(5) See Sommers and Kernan, *COMPARATIVE MARKETING SYSTEMS*.

## CHAPTER II

(1) See Clinard, *THE BLACK MARKET*.
(2) See Alderson, *DYNAMIC MARKETING BEHAVIOR*, Chapter 1.
(3) Staudt and Taylor, *A MANAGERIAL INTRODUCTION TO MARKETING*, pp. 223-224.
(4) Borch, "The Marketing Philosophy as a Way of Business Life", pp. 3-5.
(5) Adapted from Stanton, *FUNDAMENTALS OF MARKETING*, p. 109, and Woods, "Psychological Dimensions of Consumer Decisions", pp. 15-19.
(6) Tousley, et al, *PRINCIPLES OF MARKETING*, p. 14.
(7) Committee on Definitions, op. cit.
(8) Tousley, op. cit., p. 15.
(9) Ibid., p. 16.
(10) Committee on Definitions, op. cit.
(11) Ibid.
(12) Ibid.
(13) See Oxenfeldt, "Multi-Stage Approach to Pricing", pp. 125-133.
(14) See Aspinwall, "The Parallel Systems Theory", pp. 644-652.
(15) See Woods, op. cit.
(16) Stanton, op. cit., p. 77.

## CHAPTER III

(17) Gartner, *CRIME IN BUSINESS*.
(18) Dietsch, "Theft: A Hidden Tax on Consumers".

CHAPTER IV

*(19)* The Delphi technique utilizes a sequential pooling and refinement of subjective judgements to arrive at a consensus. See Fusfeld and Foster, "The Delphi Technique: Survey and Comment".

## REFERENCES


*Books*

Alderson, Wroe. *DYNAMIC MARKETING BEHAVIOR*. Homewood, IL: R.D. Irwin, 1965.

Bartels, Robert. *THE DEVELOPMENT OF MARKETING THOUGHT*. Homewood, IL: R.D. Irwin, 1961.

Clinard, Marshall. *THE BLACK MARKET*. New York: Rinehart Co, 1952.

Committee on Definitions. *MARKETING DEFINITIONS: A GLOSSARY OF MARKETING TERMS*. Chicago: American Marketing Association, 1960.

Fisk, George. *MARKETING SYSTEMS, AN INTRODUCTORY ANALYSIS*. New York: Harper and Row, 1967.

Gartner, Michael (ed.). *CRIME AND BUSINESS*. Princeton, NJ: Dow Jones, 1971.

Sommers, Montrose, and Jerome Kernan. *COMPARATIVE MARKETING SYSTEMS*. New York: Appleton-Century-Crofts, 1968.

Stanton, William J. *FUNDAMENTALS OF MARKETING*. New York: McGraw-Hill, 1964.

Staudt, Thomas and Donald Taylor. *A MANAGERIAL INTRODUCTION TO MARKETING*. Englewood Cliffs, NJ: Prentice-Hall, 1965.

Tousley, Rayburn, et al. *PRINCIPLES OF MARKETING*. New York: MacMillan, 1962.

*Articles*

Aspinwall, Leo. "The Parallel Systems Theory", *Managerial Marketing: Perspectives and Viewpoints*, William Lazer and Eugene Kelley, eds. Homewood, IL: Irwin, 1962. pp. 644-652.

Borch, Fred. "The Marketing Philosophy is a Way of Business Life", *The Marketing Concept: Its Meaning to Management*, Marketing Series No. 99. New York: American Management Association, 1957.

Dietsch, Robert. "Theft: A Hidden Tax on Consumers", *Scripps-Howard Newspapers*, July 1971.

Fusfeld, Alan and Richard Foster. "The Delphi Technique: Survey and Comment", *Business Horizons*, June 1971, pp. 63-74.

Oxenfeldt, Alfred. "A Multi-Stage Approach to Pricing", *Harvard Business Review*, July-August 1960, pp. 125-133.

Woods, Walter, "Psychological Dimensions of Consumer Decisions", *Journal of Marketing*, January 1960, pp. 15-19.

# SUGGESTED FURTHER READING

## IN THE FIELDS OF CRIME, THEFT, SELF-PROTECTION, ECONOMICS AND BLACK MARKETS

*CRIME, THEFT, POLICE SCIENCE*

Barefoot, J.K. UNDERCOVER INVESTIGATION. Charles C. Thomas, 1975.

Brickell, D. and L. Cole. BIKE THEFT. Davis Publishing Co., 1976.

Brickell, D. and L. Cole. VEHICLE THEFT INVESTIGATION. Davis Publishing Co., 1975.

Cameron, M.O. BOOSTER AND THE SNITCH - DEPARTMENT STORE SHOPLIFTING. Free Press, 1964.

David, P.R. WORLD OF THE BURGLAR - FIVE CRIMINAL LIVES. University of New Mexico Press, 1974.

Desert Publications. LOCK OUT - TECHNIQUES OF FORCED ENTRY FOR LOCKSMITHS AND LAW ENFORCEMENT. Desert Publications, 1975.

Desert Publications. LOCK PICKING SIMPLIFIED. Desert Publications, 1976.

Desert Publications. POLICE GUIDE TO LOCK PICKING AND IMPROVISED LOCK PICKS. Desert Publications, 1976.

Desert Publications. TECHNIQUE OF SAFE AND VAULT MANIPULATION. Desert Publications, 1978.

Dorski, C. POLICE MANUAL ON ILLEGAL ENTRIES. Roadrunner Publications, 1978.

Hicks, R. UNDERCOVER OPERATIONS AND PERSUASION. Charles C. Thomas, 1973.

Klockars, C.B. PROFESSIONAL FENCE. Free Press, 1974.

Letkemann, P. CRIME AS WORK. Prentice-Hall, 1973.

Lipman, M. STEALING - HOW AMERICA'S EMPLOYEES ARE STEALING THEIR COMPANIES BLIND. Harper and Row, 1973.

Loughton, F. FRAUD AND WHITE COLLAR CRIME. Elek Books Ltd., 1971.
Mentor Publications. THE ILLUSTRATED ART OF LOCK-PICKING. Mentor Publications, 1976.
Motto, C. UNDERCOVER. Charles C. Thomas, 1971.
O'Hara, C. FUNDAMENTALS OF CRIMINAL INVESTIGATION. Charles C. Thomas, 1976.
Plate, T. CRIME PAYS - AN INSIDE LOOK AT BURGLARS, CAR THIEVES, LOAN SHARKS, HIT MEN, FENCES, AND OTHER PROFESSIONALS IN CRIME. Simon and Schuster, 1975.
Rice, R. THE BUSINESS OF CRIME. Greenwood Press, 1956.
Russell, J. INVOLUNTARY REPOSSESSION. Russell & Associates, 1977.
Siljander, R. FUNDAMENTALS OF PHYSICAL SURVEILLANCE. Charles C. Thomas, 1977.
Stirling, N. YOUR MONEY OR YOUR LIFE. Bobbs-Merrill, 1974.
Tompkins, D.C. WHITE COLLAR CRIME - A BIBLIOGRAPHY. University of California Press, 1967.

*SELF-PROTECTION*

Albano, C. HIDDEN RICHES. Erco, 1974.
Hjersman, P. THE STASH BOOK - HOW TO HIDE YOUR VALUABLES. And/Or Press, 1978.
Johnson, R.A. SECURITY STORAGE CONTAINERS: DESIGN, CONSTRUCTION AND CONCEALMENT. R.A. Johnson, 1977.
Krotz, D. HOW TO HIDE ALMOST ANYTHING. Morrow, 1975.
Nelson, W., and S. Catlow. METHODS OF LONG-TERM UNDERGROUND STORAGE. Magnum Enterprises, 1976.
Nonte, G. TO STOP A THIEF. Stoeger, 1974.
Notlem, H. SECRET HIDING PLACES. Delta Press, 1977.
US Department of Transportation. CARGO SECURITY HANDBOOK FOR SHIPPERS AND RECEIVERS. US Government Printing Office, 1972.

US Department of Transportation. GUIDELINES FOR THE PHYSICAL SECURITY OF CARGO. US Government Printing Office, 1972.
Weber, T. ALARM SYSTEMS & THEFT PROTECTION. Security World, 1973.

*ECONOMICS, BLACK MARKETS*

Block, W. DEFENDING THE UNDEFENDABLE. Fleet Press, 1976.
Clinard, M. THE BLACK MARKET. Rinehart, 1952.
French, S. COMPLETE GUIDE TO THE STREET DRUG GAME. Lyle Stuart, 1976.
Green, T. THE SMUGGLING BUSINESS. Crescent Books, 1977.
Laughlin, B. JOB OPPORTUNITIES IN THE BLACK MARKET. EBLJ Publishers, 1978.
Rothbard, M. POWER AND MARKET. Institute for Humane Studies, 1970.